Procedural Generation in Godot

Learn to Generate Enjoyable Content for Your Games

Christopher Pitt

Apress®

Procedural Generation in Godot: Learn to Generate Enjoyable Content for
Your Games

Christopher Pitt
Durbanville, South Africa

ISBN-13 (pbk): 978-1-4842-8794-1
https://doi.org/10.1007/978-1-4842-8795-8

ISBN-13 (electronic): 978-1-4842-8795-8

Managing Director, Apress Media LLC: Welmoed Spahr
Acquisitions Editor: Spandana Chatterjee
Development Editor: Spandana Chatterjee
Coordinating Editor: Mark Powers

Cover designed by eStudioCalamar

Cover image by Luemen Rutkowski on Unsplash (www.unsplash.com)

Distributed to the book trade worldwide by Apress Media, LLC, 1 New York Plaza, New York, NY 10004, U.S.A. Phone 1-800-SPRINGER, fax (201) 348-4505, e-mail orders-ny@springer-sbm.com, or visit www.springeronline.com. Apress Media, LLC is a California LLC and the sole member (owner) is Springer Science + Business Media Finance Inc (SSBM Finance Inc). SSBM Finance Inc is a **Delaware** corporation.

For information on translations, please e-mail booktranslations@springernature.com; for reprint, paperback, or audio rights, please e-mail bookpermissions@springernature.com.

Apress titles may be purchased in bulk for academic, corporate, or promotional use. eBook versions and licenses are also available for most titles. For more information, reference our Print and eBook Bulk Sales web page at http://www.apress.com/bulk-sales.

Any source code or other supplementary material referenced by the author in this book is available to readers on GitHub (https://github.com/Apress). For more detailed information, please visit http://www.apress.com/source-code.

Printed on acid-free paper

This book is dedicated to my patient wife, my enthusiastic kids, and my supportive friends.

Table of Contents

About the Author

Christopher Pitt is a developer living in South Africa. He has published a bunch of indie games, many of which use procedural content generation. Most of his games have been built in the Godot engine. He also likes to bake sweet things and build wood things.

About the Technical Reviewer

Over the past 15 years, **Christopher Bray** has spent his career creating enterprise applications for hotel chains, giant analytics firms, and one of the largest businesses in the food service industry. Now, he's developing video games using Godot.

Acknowledgments

I acknowledge the folks at Apress for their tireless work and the opportunity to write this book. I'd also like to thank Christopher for his encouragement over the years and his valuable perspective as technical reviewer.

Introduction

This book is about the practical steps you can take to create games that include procedural content generation. It's been a hard six months of writing, but the games I built leading up to it were instrumental in my understanding and teaching of procedural content generation. I won't bore you with the details, except to say that the most polished games I have released are heavily featured in these pages.

You won't find a lot of complicated math, or theory about different kinds of noise generation functions. I have kept things simple and useful. If you follow along, you'll have built four games by the time you're finished. I think that's one of the best parts about this book.

It's wonderful to look back on these last six months and see how the content of this book has evolved. I started writing it with Godot 4 alpha 1 and finished writing it with Godot 4 beta 1. A lot changed during that time, so I went back through and re-built everything in beta 1 so that I was sure it would work for you. There might be small changes to the engine before launch, but the worst is behind us.

It was important for me to demonstrate this topic using Godot 4 because it's the future. I want this book to be useful to you for a long time. If you struggle with anything in it, please reach out to me.

You can find the source code for the experiments at `https://github.com/assertchris/book-experiments`

You can find the source code for each game at

- `https://github.com/assertchris/book-sokoban`

- `https://github.com/assertchris/book-bouncy-cars`

- `https://github.com/assertchris/book-invasion`

I mostly follow popular GDScript syntax conventions. Feel free to deviate from these as you like; but be careful to update the code where you've chosen different node, script, class, or file names. My habits have also changed while writing the book; but things are mostly consistent following the most recent set of edits. All source code used in the book can be downloaded from `http://github.com/apress/procedural-generation-godot`.

I suggest you learn the basics of GDScript before attempting to master this topic. GDQuest has a brilliant introductory application you can try: `https://gdquest.github.io/learn-gdscript`. I explain things as simply as possible, but you'll have an easier time if you already know some programming concepts.

CHAPTER 1

Hand-Crafted Content vs. Procedural Content

There are many popular games that place the player in sprawling worlds. Examples of this are World of Warcraft and Red Dead Redemption. An interesting thing about these games is their hand-crafted content. A team of designers have worked to create every hill and valley. A computer made none of it via an algorithm.

Hand-crafted content is the kind of content that is intentionally made. This could be someone drawing a game character, or creating a 3D model of a car. It also includes the design of the game world, or smaller sections contained in it.

In this book, we're going to focus mostly on designing the game world. If you've ever played a strategy game, the concept of a map will be familiar to you. It's the space in which you build your buildings and command your units.

There are other games that build on this concept, though it might not be immediately clear. Each of Super Mario Bros' worlds is a kind of map. The race tracks in Need for Speed are maps. If it's a space you, as the player, can move around in, you can think of it as a map.

There's a level of quality in hand-crafted content that only human hands can achieve. A predictable map also leads to environments and events that feel more natural to the player.

Let's take a closer look at a game built on hand-crafted maps.

Example: Limbo

Limbo is a puzzle-platformer game, released in 2010. You wake up, alone, and need to solve puzzles to understand what is happening to you. It's particularly memorable for its black-and-white color palette and sound design.

© Christopher Pitt 2023
C. Pitt, *Procedural Generation in Godot*, https://doi.org/10.1007/978-1-4842-8795-8_1

Sailing in Limbo

Limbo is full of interesting puzzles, each more difficult than the last. There are stretches of gameplay, where the player must navigate the world in limited time. This combines with stretches where the player can relax and sightsee.

This is possible due to the order of sections of the map and predictable layout of each section. Every playthrough is similar, and later playthroughs are easier if you recall the solutions to puzzles.

Running from a spider in Limbo

Procedural Content Generation

When algorithms generate content, instead of a designer, we call this procedural generation. All procedural generation begins with a designer creating content, but the algorithm takes over at some point.

This *content* can take many forms:

- Basic layouts that the algorithm can combine and rearrange

- The functions that create these arrangements

- Checks to ensure the generated content is acceptable

- Functions that spawn player characters, nonplayable characters, and enemies into the generated areas

These will be the main focus of this book. This isn't an exhaustive list of things considered procedural generation, but it's a start.

Generated content has the potential to create limitless replayability for your games. A solo game developer can delegate content creation to a machine and focus on other parts of their game. The flip side to this is that generated content can also be messy, imprecise, and buggy.

It'll also be harder to design the pacing, events, and triggers of your game well. You'll need to balance these concerns to create a robust set of tools.

Let's take a look at a game that demonstrates balanced procedural content generation.

Example: Oxygen Not Included

Oxygen Not Included is a colony management simulator, released in 2017. You start off managing three colonists, with varying skills and characteristics. I enjoy the humorous interactions they have with each other and the perilous situations they can find themselves in.

Supervising in Oxygen Not Included

There are two main kinds of starting data that Oxygen Not Included uses to generate its maps from:

- The starting area, where everything is safe and there's a bit of water and oxygen

- The configuration of a handful of structures that later aid the player in expansion

The rest is a rich generation algorithm that builds beautiful worlds to play in. Every playthrough is different. That is, unless you recreate the exact same world on purpose.

Selecting a seed in Oxygen Not Included

Newer versions of the game have added more world options, but it's still generated content at the core. When you start a new game, you're faced with an array of questions:

- "How will this new map look?"

- "What geysers will I have around me?"

- "Will this map be easy or hard to survive in?"

This is what makes the game so enjoyable and replayable. It's all thanks to the robust content generation algorithm.

How Much of Each?

Perhaps you're wondering how much content you should design and how much you should generate. It's a good question, without an easy answer.

Crafted content will usually be higher quality than generated content, but it's also more expensive to make. If you're building something on your own, you want to figure out how much of it you can generate.

Same thing if you're entering a game jam.

We've already seen a good example of how you could mix them in Oxygen Not Included. There will be sections of your maps that you want to be safe, or to host a special event. You should craft these to avoid complexity.

You could generate the rest, or you could even use crafted sections combined in random ways. There are many examples of this last approach.

Example: Diablo 2

Diablo 2 is an action role-playing game, released in 2000. It's a story-rich game where you are a warrior of light, battling an army of darkness. It's memorable for its dark atmosphere and gothic aesthetic.

The remastered version was released in 2021.

Slaying demons in Diablo 2: Resurrected

Diablo 2 has a mix of crafted and generated content. It takes place in five main locations of a fictional world.

Each location (called act) has its own look and feel. The acts are also broken up into a set order of smaller sections (or zones), each with their own visual traits.

For example, act two has a desert theme. You begin your adventuring alongside sand dunes and decaying limestone structures. One of the zones takes you deep into an underground tunnel system. Another takes you into the city's dark sewer system.

Exploring the deserts of act two in Diablo 2: Resurrected

These areas are full of interesting crafted assets, randomly placed and weighted. There's only one entrance to that underground tunnel system, but you'll have to discover where that is each time you load the game.

The game has a fast-travel mechanic, which you access through randomly placed teleport platforms. Finding these, and the entrances to special story areas, is a core part of the game's mechanics.

Yet each act starts you off in a crafted safe area. These are always the same, so you can quickly navigate them on your frequent trips "back to town."

Starting (safe) zone of act five in Diablo 2: Resurrected

The typical structure of each act and zone varies, but here is a non-exhaustive list of zones in act one:

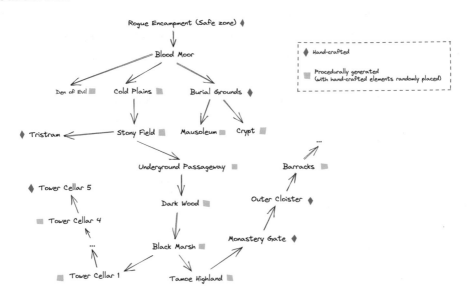

Crafted and generated areas of act one in Diablo 2: Resurrected

There are definitely more generated sections of the game, but the crafted sections help to connect them together. They are the setting for important events in the story.

Most of the enemies you'll encounter are randomly generated, but each type belongs to a specific zone or act. You encounter simple skeletons and zombies in act one, lightning beetles in act two, tree ents in act three, etc.

Some zones have a high chance to spawn special enemies. In the Stony Field of act one, you will always encounter a special enemy called Rakanishu. He guards the entrance to Tristram and has a lightning attack.

Each act has a handful of these special enemies, as well as a final boss. The final bosses are also in crafted locations. Generated loot drops from slain enemies, with a small selection of crafted items, called legendaries.

Where We Go from Here

We're going to build a toolset that balances crafted and generated content. That means we'll create some crafted assets and combine them in ways that can lead to random configurations.

We'll learn how to build explicit seeding systems, as seen in Oxygen Not Included, so that friends can share experiences with us.

We'll learn about things like tile maps and nodes and how to make them interact. We'll learn about how to inspect generated maps to be able to figure out how to answer questions like

- "What is the right direction to move it?"

- "How do I get over to that part of the generated map?"

- "Where is a good place to spawn enemies?"

We'll learn how to make click-to-move, keyboard-based, and path-based movement.

As we learn more tricks, we'll recreate games from different genres. By the time you're done reading this book, you'll have made four different 2D games.

Buckle up!

CHAPTER 2

Generating with Nodes

In the previous chapter, we talked about why you'd want to generate content rather than craft it. It's time to get into the code of things.

In this chapter, we're going to create a fresh project where we can experiment. We'll follow this up by creating nodes via code and randomizing their behavior.

My version of Godot might differ from yours since I'm writing this a few months before you read it. I'm using an early version of Godot 4, so as long as you're using Godot 4, we should be good. You can find installation instructions on the Godot website.

Setting Up a New Project

Launch Godot 4. If it's the first time, you'll see a message asking if you'd like to import an example project. We'll ignore this and create a blank project:

C. Pitt, *Procedural Generation in Godot*, https://doi.org/10.1007/978-1-4842-8795-8_2

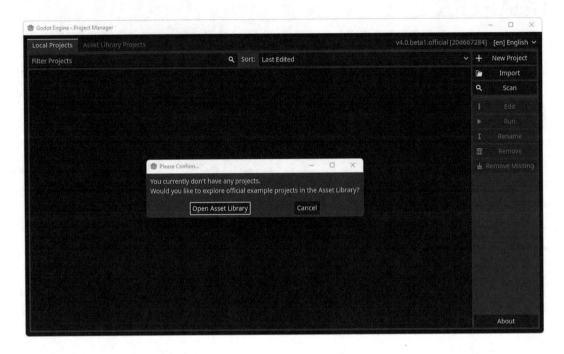

Opening Godot 4 for the first time

Clicking *Cancel* ➤ *New Project* will show a dialog asking for details about your project:

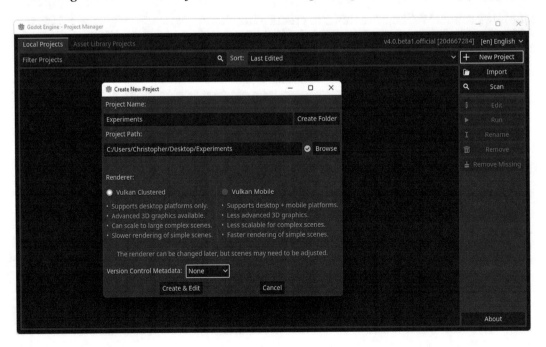

Creating a new project

There's not a lot we need to change here. Give your project a name, and set version control metadata to *None*. Whatever rendering engine you pick will work for the purposes of this project.

Version control is a good thing, but it's not in the scope of this book. If you're familiar with Git, then feel free to use that. I won't be going into detail about how it works or how to set it up.

Clicking *Create & Edit* will take you to the default editor view. I usually do the same things when starting a new game to create a solid base:

- I start by creating a base Screen scene, with a `MarginContainer` as a main node.

- I inherit this scene to create screens, including one in which the gameplay happens.

- I move automatically created configuration files and icons to folders that represent their types.

Here's what that Screen scene looks like:

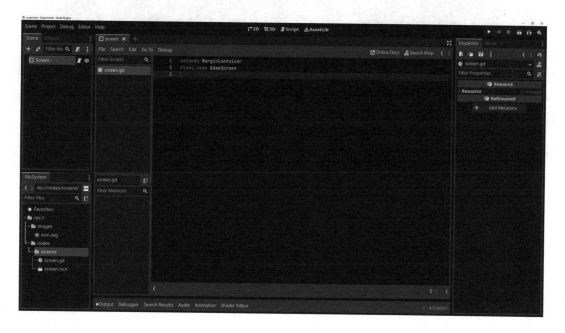

Creating the base Screen scene

I prefix my class names so that there's no risk of their name conflicting with a built-in class. It's rare for this to happen, but a prefix avoids the issue altogether.

If we switch to the 2D editor tab, we can select the `MarginContainer` node and expand it to fill all the available screen space. This means that all our screens will fill the available screen space.

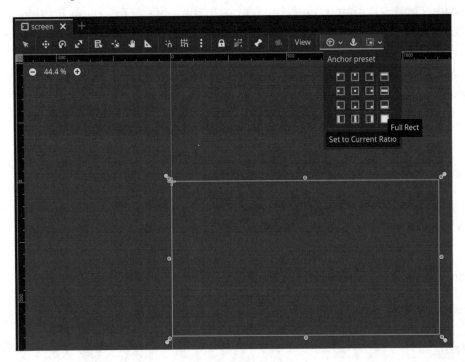

Expanding the `MarginContainer` node

Since this class has a name, we can inherit from it without a path to the file in our code. Let me show you what a subclass of `GameScreen` looks like:

Extending a class

I recommend spending some time looking through the editor settings to get it set up the way you like to use it. I sometimes increase the editor interface size, but you can do what feels natural for you.

To get to this point, I selected the *Scene* ➤ *New Inherited Scene* menu option and selected the `screen.tscn` file I created as the parent scene. After selecting and renaming the Screen node, I went to *Script* ➤ *New Script*. That shows this dialog:

Creating a new script

We saw this dialog when we attached a script to the Screen node. This time, we should change where it says `MarginContainer` to `GameScreen`. Clicking *Create* will make the new script. You should see both files (`play_screen.tscn` and `play_screen.gd`) in the file explorer, on the left side of the screen.

I like to use `MarginContainer` as the main node because some mobile devices have camera notches. This requires that we resize the game so that it isn't hidden behind a notch. We can code the `MarginContainer` to add padding after the game starts.

When you click the play button, at the top right of the screen, Godot will ask you to set a default scene. Pick the PlayScreen as the default scene:

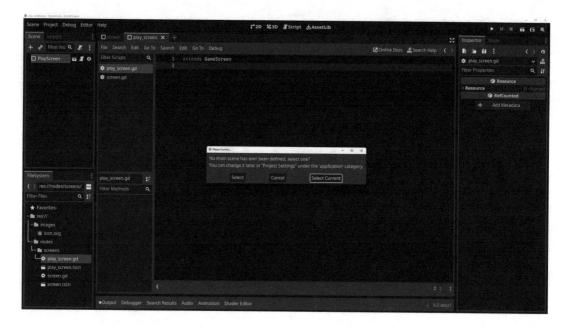

Configuring the default scene

Loading Experiments

We're going to use a single experiment project for most of the code we're going to write. We need a way to load different experiments as we work on them. One way to achieve this is to put each experiment in a Node2D node and center that in the play screen.

Let's add a CenterContainer and Control to the MarginContainer:

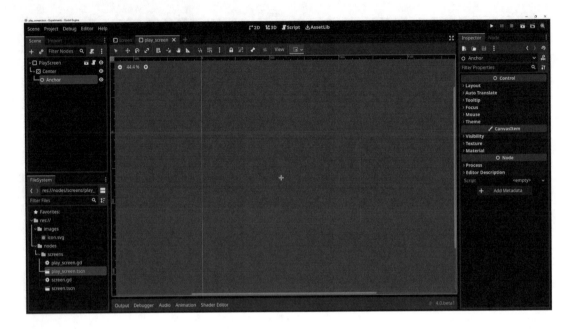

Centering experiments in the PlayScreen

Now, we can make each experiment a Node2D scene, starting with the base GameExperiment:

Creating the GameExperiment class

We can extend this for our first experiment, which is going to be about randomizing nodes. We can call this the NodesExperiment:

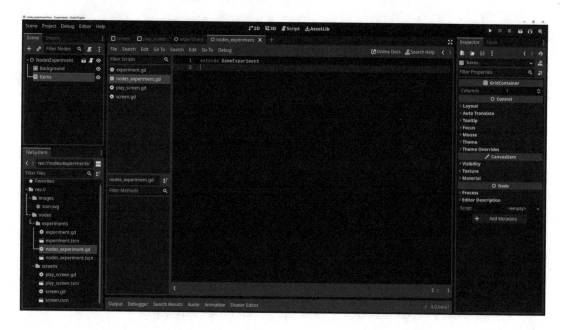

Creating the NodesExperiment class

I've also created a 200 × 200 ColorRect background and a 200 × 200 GridContainer, into which we're going to create 25 child nodes. We should set the GridContainer node to have 5 columns.

The Node2D experiment node will be in the center of the Anchor node, so we should set the size of the background and grid to -100 × -100.

There are a few ways we could bring this experiment into PlayScreen:

- load("res://nodes/experiments/nodes-experiment.gd")

- preload("res://nodes/experiments/nodes-experiment.gd")

But both of these suffer from an annoying problem. In fact, it's the same problem we've tried to avoid with custom class names. When files move, those strings aren't updated.

The safest way to reference other nodes is by class name, or exported variables. Here's what I mean:

This is from nodes/screens/play_screen.gd

```
extends GameScreen

@export var experiment_scene : PackedScene

@onready var _anchor := $Center/Anchor

func _ready() -> void:
    var experiment = experiment_scene.instantiate()
    _anchor.add_child(experiment)
```

Godot 4 uses @export and @onready to hint that these variables need special handling:

- @export variables are available through the property inspector.

- @onready variables resolve after the parent node is ready.

The instantiate method creates a new instance of the experiment scene so that we can add it to the scene.

_anchor starts with an underscore because I want to hint that it is private to this script. The underscore doesn't affect functionality. It's a pattern that is popular in the Python and GDScript programming languages.

When you go back to the visual editor and select PlayScreen, you should see the variable on the right side of the screen. We call this area the Property Inspector:

Finding the exported variable

Clicking on *Empty* will show a couple of ways to pick the experiment. We can drag the NodesExperiment scene onto the drop-down, and it would link them; but this might not be practical in a huge project. A better option is to click *Empty* ➤ *Quick Load*.

This will display a searchable list of PackedScene nodes to select from:

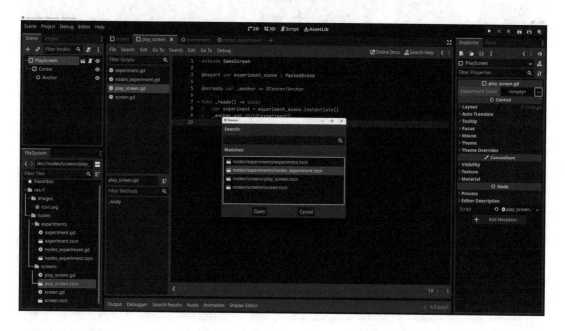

Selecting the NodesExperiment scene from a searchable list

Once selected and saved, you can click the play button and see the experiment as the game launches:

Launching the experiment

This a nice, reusable system for packaging and loading our future experiments. We're going to have another eight of them; so we're definitely going to get some mileage out of this system.

Creating Nodes via Script

Let's create a new scene, which we'll randomize the behavior of. You can imagine this as a part of the game's environment, a decoration, like a tree or rock. We're going to keep things simple and use a ColorRect:

Creating the doodad class

ColorRect is a good node type to choose here because the experiment will show it in a GridContainer. It's not required for all your decorations, unless you're also going to display them in a similar way.

Set *Layout ➤ Transform ➤ Size* to 40 × 40 and *Layout ➤ Container Sizing* to expand × expand. Then, we need to "import" it in a similar way to what we did for the experiments:

This is from nodes/experiments/nodes_experiments.gd

```
extends GameExperiment

@export var doodad_scene : PackedScene

@onready var _items := $Items

func _ready() -> void:
    for i in range(25):
        var doodad = doodad_scene.instantiate()
        _items.add_child(doodad)
```

Now, when running the game, we should see a grid of Doodad classes:

Testing the grid rendering

If you're using a Sprite2D for your decoration, you can swap the GridContainer for position or global_position attributes. We'll get around to doing that in later chapters. For now, what's more important is to talk about how we add randomization to this Doodad class.

Randomizing Behavior

There are a couple types of randomization we could use:

- Seeded – Generation with a fixed seed

- Unseeded – Generation based on a random seed

Both are a kind of seeded generation, but the difference is whether we want to know and control the seed or not. For now, we're not going to control the seed. Chapter 6 is when we'll start doing that.

Let's create a script on the Doodad class and randomize the colors of the ColorRect:

This is from nodes/experiments/nodes_experiment/doodad.gd

```
extends ColorRect

func _ready() -> void:
    color = Color(
        randf_range(0.0, 1.0),
        randf_range(0.0, 1.0),
        randf_range(0.0, 1.0)
    )
```

Godot 4 automatically calls the randomize function, so we don't need to call it ourselves. This function seeds the built-in random number generator, so it's not outputting predictable values.

The randf_range(min, max) function returns a random float value between minimum and maximum values.

There are many rand* functions to choose from:

- randf

- randf_range

- randi

- randi_range

- randfn

The randf function is shorthand for randf_range(0.0, 1.0). The randi_range(min, max) function is shorthand for randi() % 100, where min is 0 and max is 99. If that's a lot, don't worry. We're mostly going to deal in integers; and we'll see plenty of examples that will help clear things up.

Creating Realism with Randomization

So, we can randomize the colors of the squares; but how do we use this knowledge to do something more useful. Say we wanted to make the squares green (for trees) or brown (for rocks) or transparent. We could use randf* or randi* to generate a number and then do different things based on what that number is.

Something like this:

This is from nodes/experiments/nodes_experiment/doodad.gd

```
extends ColorRect

func _ready() -> void:
    var number = randf()

    if number > 0.9:
        color = Color.DARK_GREEN
    elif number > 0.7:
        color = Color.SADDLE_BROWN
    else:
        color = Color.TRANSPARENT
```

We start by generating a random number between 0.0 and 1.0. Then we compare it and only make the ColorRect green when the number is above 0.9. This creates a one-in-ten chance that the ColorRect will be green. If that one-in-ten chance fails, there's a three-in-ten chance that ColorRect will be brown.

Trees and rocks with randomization

We can make subtle changes to this, but the general idea will remain the same for all the node randomization we do in the rest of the book.

Summary

In this chapter, we learned about how to create new nodes and randomize values in Godot 4. We set up a new project and covered some habits I generally recommend for structuring project code.

Take some time to experiment with the rand functions. See if you can figure out how to use different thresholds for your random values.

Try to use Sprite nodes, showing and hiding as appropriate.

In the following chapter, we're going to take these techniques further with tile sets.

CHAPTER 3

Generating with Tiles

In the previous chapter, we created and manipulated **nodes** using scripts. It's one of two popular ways to manipulate the visuals of a game. In this chapter, we're going to look at the other, which is creating and manipulating **tiles** via scripts.

We need to start in the visual editor, where we'll learn how to set up tiles and terrains. These are useful for hand-crafted content, and mastering them will save a ton of time and code.

Creating Tile Sets

Tile maps are visual areas made out of little squares or tiles. Take a look at the following image:

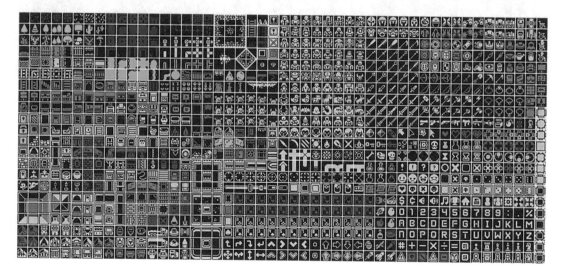

This is from https://kenney.nl/assets/bit-pack

© Christopher Pitt 2023
C. Pitt, *Procedural Generation in Godot*, https://doi.org/10.1007/978-1-4842-8795-8_3

This is a tile sheet. It's a collection of small tiles packed in a way that makes them easier to use when creating maps for games. There are many tiles in this tile sheet that are perfect for creating a map. Let's create a new experiment that uses them!

Download and extract the asset pack, and copy **colored.png** into the **images** folder, in the experiment project. Then, create an inherited scene, based on the GameExperiment class. Follow this up by adding a new node, below the root node, called a *TileMap*:

Creating a TileMap

Attach a script to the new scene, like we did in the previous chapter. This script should inherit from the GameExperiment class. TileMap nodes are the mechanism for **how** we draw tiles. They need a TileSet resource, which is **what** gets drawn in them. We can share tile sets between many TileMap nodes, but that's an exercise for later.

Click on the *Empty* drop-down next to *Tile Set* and select *New TileSet*. You'll see a grid appear in the 2D editor.

Editing the new TileSet

This grid is where we'll draw the tiles, but we first need to define tiles in the tile set. I found this part to be a bit tricky when I first tried it. The *TileSet* editor button at the bottom of the screen wasn't showing up for me. If this happens for you, select another node, like TilesExperiment, and click back on the TileMap node. You should now see the *TileSet* tab at the bottom of the screen.

The image we're using has 16 × 16 pixel tiles, so we don't have to change the default tile size for the TileMap node. If we wanted to, we could click on *TileSet* and change *Tile Size* values that show up in the property inspector.

Let's create a new *Atlas* by clicking the plus button and selecting *Atlas*. Then, click *Texture* ➤ *Quick Load*. Select colored.png. Godot will ask if you want it to *automatically create tiles in the atlas*, to which you can say *no*:

Selecting a texture

The image we're using has gaps in between the tiles. Adjust the *Separation* values to account for these gaps. Values of 1 × 1 should do the trick. Highlight a few tiles for us to use:

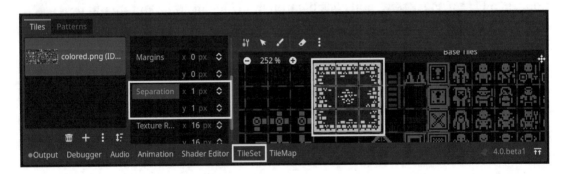

Highlighting wall tiles

Now, we can draw on the grid with a tile selected. When we want to change the tile we're drawing with, we can select a new one from the set that we highlighted:

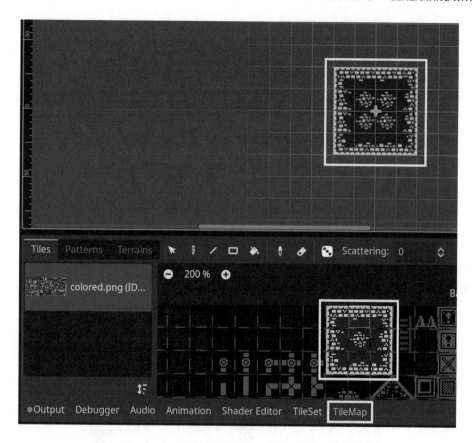

Drawing tiles by hand

Modifying Tiles with Code

We can also draw tiles on the grid using code. Let's create a script for the
TilesExperiment node and set these tiles with it:

This is from nodes/experiments/tiles_experiment.gd

```
extends GameExperiment

@onready var _tile_map := $TileMap as TileMap

func _ready() -> void:
    _tile_map.clear()
```

33

```
var tiles := [
    [Vector2(0, -2), Vector2(19, 0)],
    [Vector2(1, -2), Vector2(19, 0)],
    [Vector2(2, -2), Vector2(20, 0)],
    [Vector2(2, -1), Vector2(20, 1)],
    [Vector2(2, 0), Vector2(20, 1)],
]

for tile in tiles:
    _tile_map.set_cell(0, tile[0], 2, tile[1])
```

There are quite a few methods available on a TileMap node, but we only need three for now. The first is to clear tiles that we have already drawn on the grid. This could be tiles drawn via other scripts or drawn by hand.

The second method is to draw the intended tile in the intended cell location. These numbers can be confusing, so let's break it down.

The first Vector2 in each row of the tiles array is the grid position of the cell we want to draw on. At the center of the screen (or origin), the grid starts at 0,0.

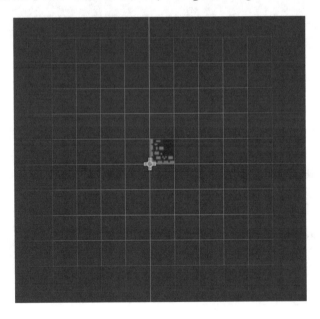

Drawing tiles from the origin

This means a cell on the top left of the one pictured is going to have the grid position of -1, -1.

The second Vector2 in each row of tiles is the location in the atlas of the tile that we want to draw. If you mouse over the tile, you'll see this number pop up:

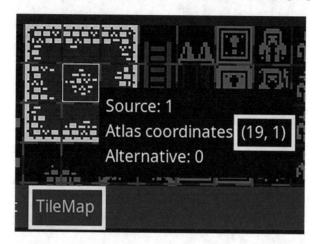

Hovering over a tile to see the atlas coordinate

In the set_cell method call, we're telling the tile map we want to draw the cells on layer 0. We're telling it that the tile the source is 2.

You can see the source when you hover over a tile in the tile map inspector. Source is the numeric identifier for the atlas of tiles we're drawing from.

Using Terrains

Drawing large configurations of tiles can be a tedious process, especially when the different tiles represent walls facing a different direction.

Godot has a feature called terrains that can do a lot of this work for us. To set up a new terrain, go to the TileMap node properties and click on the *TileSet* to go to the TileSet's properties:

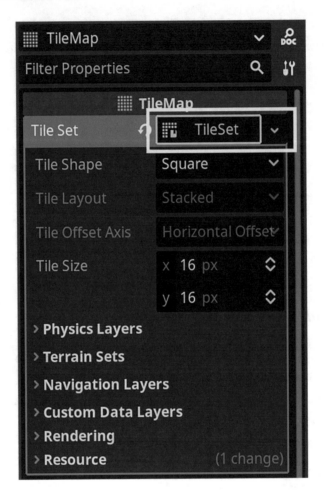

Drilling down to TileSet properties

Then, find the terrains tab and add a new terrain:

Adding a new terrain

Select *Match Corners and Sides* as a *Terrain Set ➤ Mode*. Next, go to the *TileSet* tab and click the paint brush icon. You'll see *Paint Properties* with the choice of what you want to paint:

Painting terrains

Picking which terrain to add tiles

Pick the terrain and color in the parts of each tile that should connect to each other:

Painting bit masks

You might want to deselect the bit you've selected in error. Change *Terrain* ➤ *Walls* to *Terrain* ➤ *No terrain* and left click on the bit you want to remove. We can go back to *TileMap* ➤ *Terrains* ➤ *Terrain Set 0* ➤ *walls,* and paint with *Connect mode* selected:

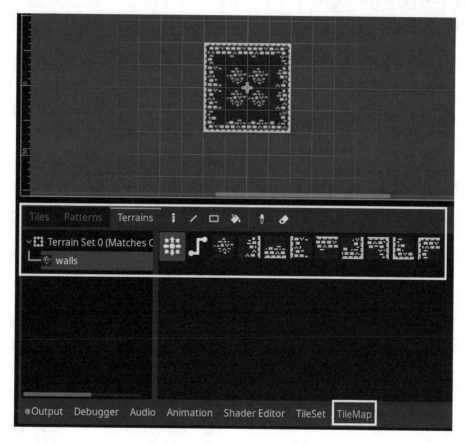

Drawing tiles with terrains

Using Terrains with Code

Scripting terrains is actually easier than scripting individual tiles. Instead of calling set_ cell for each cell we want to paint, we can create an array of cells to paint and tell the tile map which terrain to use:

This is from nodes/experiments/tiles_experiment.gd

```
var cells : Array[Vector2i] = [
    Vector2i(-1, 0),
    Vector2i(0, 0),
    Vector2i(-1, 1),
    Vector2i(0, 1),
]

_tile_map.set_cells_terrain_connect(0, cells, 0, 0, false)
```

Drawing terrains with code

Summary

In this chapter, we learned about TileMap, TileSet, and the terrain interfaces. We saw how to draw tiles into the cell grid by hand and also via script. We're going to use these techniques in the following chapter when we build our first game!

CHAPTER 4

Recreating Sokoban

We're well on our way to learning how to generate great procedural content for our games. It's a good time to cement what we've learned so far by using those skills to make a game.

In the previous two chapters, we learned about how to make and use nodes and tile sets. We're going to use both of those to recreate a classic game, called Sokoban.

Sokoban is actually a whole genre of games, but I want us to focus on a simple implementation of the version published around 1980.

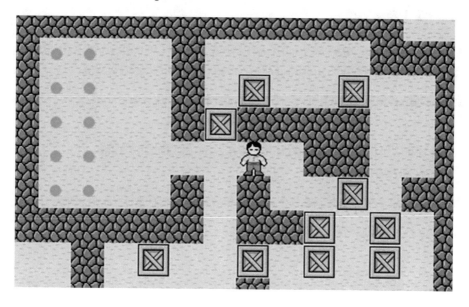

Pushing crates onto dots

The game is about pushing crates on to dots. It's a puzzle game, where the order of moves is important.

© Christopher Pitt 2023
C. Pitt, *Procedural Generation in Godot*, https://doi.org/10.1007/978-1-4842-8795-8_4

We're not going to make a game that is ready for release, though you're welcome to do that if you like. Instead, I want us to achieve the following few goals:

- Creating a level selection menu

- Designing two or three levels, representing the layout of each level in an array

- Using these arrays to draw tiles and nodes

- Implementing player movement

- Allowing the player to move boxes

- Detecting when the boxes are over the dots to signal a win state

Let's get started.

Creating Levels

We can follow the same process we did when setting up the experiment project. After creating the new project, we can create the following nodes and scripts:

1. A template Screen node, with the corresponding GameScreen class script

2. A LevelSelectionScreen node, with a script that extends GameScreen

3. A PlayScreen node, with another script that extends GameScreen

Your folders and files should resemble this:

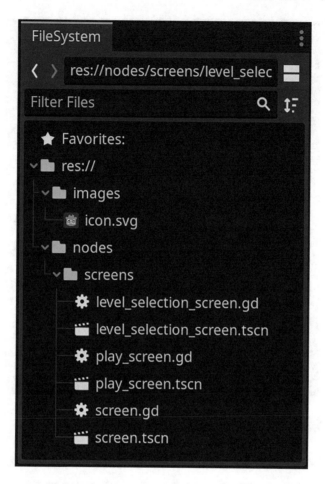

Starting with three screens

Next, let's think about how we want to design each level. It would be good for us to
have a template resource that defines a few types and properties common to each level.
We do this by creating a new folder and adding a new script to it:

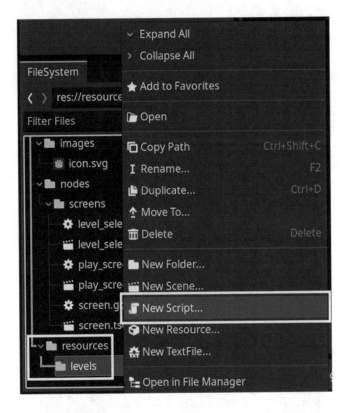

Creating new scripts

This script should inherit from the Resource class, and we can save it as level.gd:

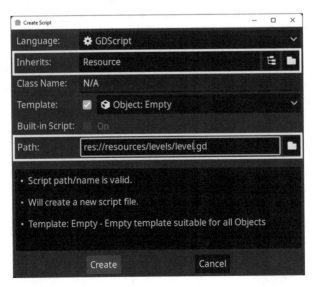

Inheriting from Resource

This class should have properties that describe each level. We can use enums (which are lists of possible values) to define the kinds of objects we can draw:

This is from resources/levels/level.gd

```
extends Resource
class_name GameLevel

enum types {
    wall_top_left,
    wall_top,
    wall_top_right,
    wall_right,
    wall_bottom_right,
    wall_bottom,
    wall_bottom_left,
    wall_left,
    empty,
    player,
    crate,
    dot,
    door,
}

@export var name := "New level"

@export var width := 7

@export var layout : Array[types] = [
    types.wall_top_left, types.wall_top, types.wall_top, types.wall_top,
types.wall_top, types.wall_top, types.wall_top_right,
    types.wall_left, types.empty, types.empty, types.empty, types.empty,
types.empty, types.wall_right,
    types.wall_left, types.empty, types.empty, types.empty, types.empty,
types.empty, types.wall_right,
    types.wall_left, types.empty, types.empty, types.empty, types.empty,
types.empty, types.wall_right,
```

```
    types.wall_left, types.empty, types.empty, types.empty, types.empty,
types.empty, types.wall_right,
    types.wall_left, types.empty, types.empty, types.empty, types.empty,
types.empty, types.wall_right,
    types.wall_bottom_left, types.wall_bottom, types.wall_bottom, types.
wall_bottom, types.wall_bottom, types.wall_bottom, types.wall_bottom_right,
    ]
```

Each level needs a name so that exported property makes sense to add. The couple that follow it need some explanation, though. I want us to take a step back and think about how levels can be build using algorithms.

The algorithm we need is one that reads level layouts from an array and draws on a tile map or with nodes. That's why each item in the layout array is a type of block, which can represent a wall or a crate or even the player. width tells our drawing code how many blocks are in each row of the layout.

This layout array depicts an empty room surrounded by walls. It's an example to show what kind of data we expect level designers to come up with. Custom resources like this are useful to let us define a custom data type that we can reference in other nodes.

Instead of linking this script to a scene, we need to create instances of this custom resource with the data values customized. We can right-click the resources/levels folder and select the *New Resource* option:

Creating a new resource in the file explorer

And we can find the custom resource in the list of possible resources to create by searching for its name:

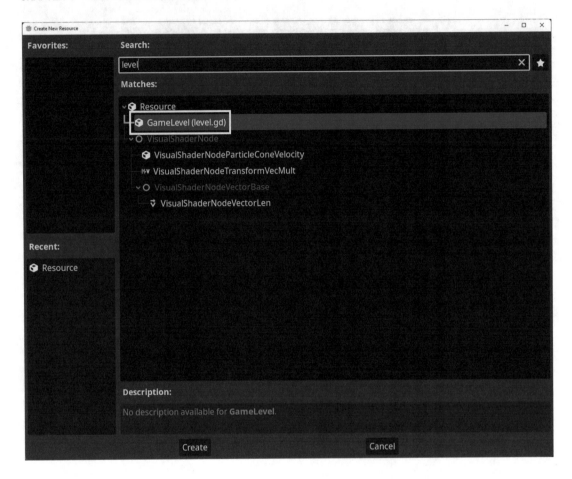

Selecting our custom resource

This instance of our custom resource has properties we can set in the property inspector. We can decide how many blocks wide each level will be and create an array of block types that is a multiple of that *Width*. I've chosen to define a layout that is the same size as the example – seven blocks wide and seven blocks high:

Defining the layout of a level in blocks

It might be tricky to think of the layout in this way. I'd suggest, if you're having trouble, that you use a bit of grid paper to design the level before creating this resource.

0	1	2	3	4	5	6
7	8	9	10	11	12	13
14	15	16	17	18	19	20
21	22	23	24	25	26	27
28	29	30	31	32	33	34
35	36	37	38	39	40	41
42	43	44	45	46	47	48

Array indices for your 7 × 7 grid layouts

Take some time to design two or three of these levels, and create their corresponding resource files. We'll need them in the next section.

Selecting a Level

By now, we've created some levels and the placeholder for a level selection screen. Let's connect the two so that we can launch our levels from the level selection screen.

First, we'll need to export a list of levels from our level selection screen and draw buttons on the screen for each level. We can set up some nodes to make the layout of this easier:

Layout nodes for easier button placement

We need to write a script that will load each configured level resource as a button that we can use to start that level:

This is from nodes/screens/level_selection_screen.gd

```
extends GameScreen

@export var levels : Array[Resource]

@onready var _vbox := $CenterContainer/VBoxContainer

func _ready() -> void:
    for level in levels:
        var new_button = Button.new()
        new_button.text = level.name
```

```
new_button.connect("pressed", func():
    print("load level: " + level.name)
)

_vbox.add_child(new_button)
```

We can export an array of the levels we've designed, so we can link them through the property inspector. When the level selection screen loads, we loop through each of the linked levels. We create a new button for each, adding it to the VBoxContainer we set up.

We can also define a lambda to execute when the player presses a button. Switch back to the *2D* tab, go to the property inspector, and link the levels you've designed:

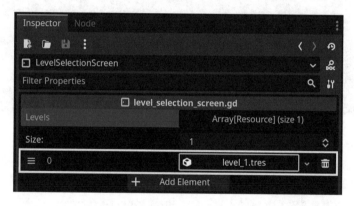

Linking our levels

Now is a good time to launch the game to see if everything is working as expected. Select the level selection screen as the default screen to load on startup, and click on the buttons!

Clicking all the buttons

If you don't see any buttons, or they don't print text to the console when you click on them, then something's wrong. Go back and look for syntax errors.

Switching Screens

Changing screens can be a bit of a mission if you've never done it before. It's a balance between flexibility and simplicity. We want the mechanism we create and use to be extensible, so we can add more screens without many changes to code. We also want the functions we call to be simple to use.

A good way to achieve this is to store a lookup table of screens in a global Constants class. Let's make a new folder and a new scene from a Node node:

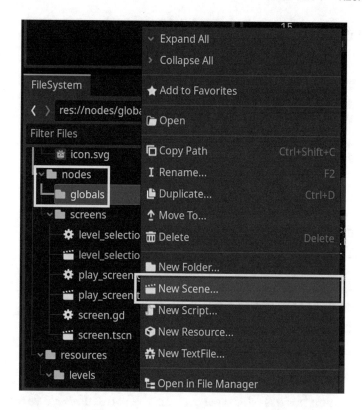

Creating a new Node scene

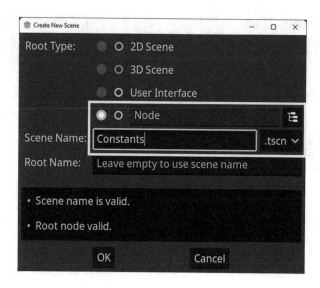

Selecting the main node of the new scene

This is from nodes/globals/constants.gd

```
extends Node
class_name Types

enum screens {
    none,
    level_selection,
    play,
}

@export var level_selection_scene : PackedScene
@export var play_scene : PackedScene

@onready var screen_scenes := {
    screens.level_selection: level_selection_scene,
    screens.play: play_scene,
}
```

We can attach this script to the main node of a new scene file, which we'll autoload in a minute. This main node is where we can link the two scenes we've exported using the property inspector.

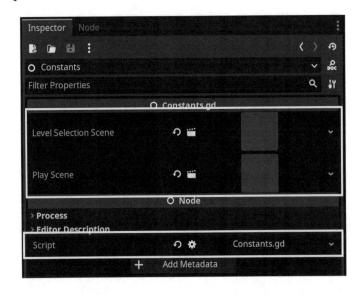

Linking to our different screen scenes

Linking them as exported properties makes it easy to replace the scenes or rename the files, without breaking hard-coded paths in code. We can use these constants in another global scene. This new scene remembers the current screen and swaps it out with new screens. Create another Node scene, called Screens, and attach another script to it:

This is from nodes/globals/screens.gd

```
extends Node

var root = null
var current_screen : Types.screens
var current_screen_node : GameScreen
var is_changing_screen := false

func _ready() -> void:
    root = get_tree().get_root()
    current_screen_node = root.get_children().back()

func change_screen(new_screen: Types.screens) -> void:
    if is_changing_screen:
        return

    is_changing_screen = true

    var new_screen_node : GameScreen = Constants.screen_scenes[new_screen].
    instantiate()
    load_new_screen(new_screen_node, new_screen)

func load_new_screen(new_screen_node: GameScreen, new_screen: Types.
screens) -> void:
    current_screen_node.queue_free()
    root.add_child(new_screen_node)

    current_screen = new_screen
    current_screen_node = new_screen_node

    is_changing_screen = false
```

We'll call the change_screen method shortly. Before we do, we need one last global scene. It needs to store the current level we intend to play so that the play screen can draw the appropriate play space. Create yet another Node scene and attached script, called Variables:

This is from nodes/globals/variables.gd

```
extends Node
```

```
var current_level : GameLevel
```

We need to autoload these three scenes by going to *Project* ➤ *Project Settings* ➤ *Autoload*:

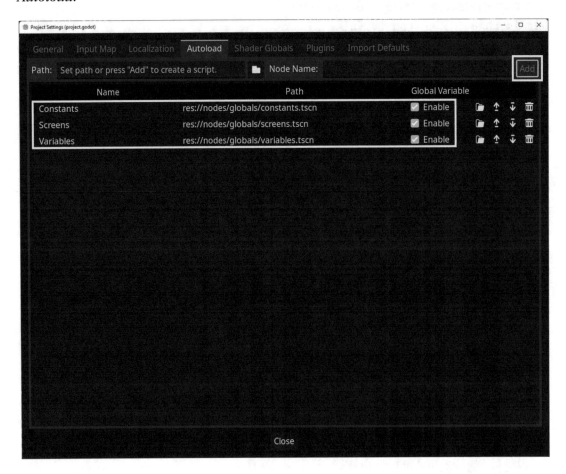

Loading our globals

To be super clear about the structure of these files, here is what my file explorer looks like:

Globals in the file explorer

Instead of printing to the debug console; we can now store the desired level, and change to the play screen:

This is from nodes/screens/level_selection_screen.gd

```
new_button.connect("pressed", func():
    Variables.current_level = level
    Screens.change_screen(Types.screens.play)
)
```

Globals and Other Mischief

Before we move on, I want to talk a bit about globals in our code. Some people will tell you to avoid autoloaded scenes because they can cause problems. I don't think this practice is as bad as they say.

The approach we've used is perfect for our needs, and we should continue to use it. This book is about procedural content generation, and not about the perils of using globals, after all.

The only other thing I want to mention is that we can't refer to types defined in a global to type-hint variables in another script. That's why I gave the Constants script a class name of Types.

The following would have resulted in an error:

```
func change_screen(new_screen: Constants.screens) -> void:
```

...because Godot cannot verify the type of `Constants.screens` at compile time. We can autoload a scene with one global name and reference its types using a different class name.

It's a trick I've only found useful in this situation. It might be cleaner to separate the types out from the constants so that we autoload one and not the other, but I'm not going to do that.

Drawing Levels

Our play screen can use the current level data to draw the level's tiles and nodes. I think it would be fun to use another kenney.nl asset pack for this project. You can find this one at `https://kenney.nl/assets/sokoban`:

Kenney's take on Sokoban sprites

Download and extract the asset pack, and copy `Tilesheet/sokoban_tilesheet.png` into the project's `images` folder. Next, create a `TileMap` and a `Node2D`. You can even create the `TileSet` resource using your knowledge from the previous chapter:

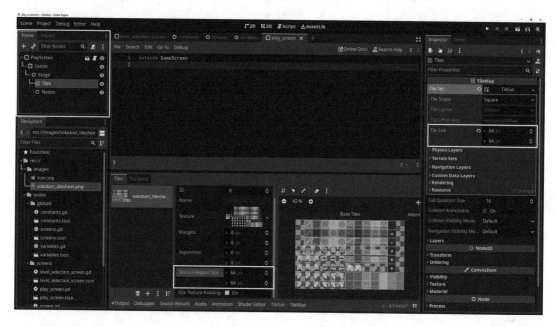

Setting the stage for drawing our levels

I typically change the default node names so they are more descriptive or less verbose. In this case, I've chosen the following names:

- `CenterContainer` → `Center`
- `Control` → `Stage`
- `TileMap` → `Tiles`
- `Node2D` → `Nodes`

If your tiles are fuzzy after importing, set *CanvasItem* → *Filter* to *Nearest*. You'll also need to adjust the tile size to 64 × 64 pixels, where I've highlighted.

By now, we've covered the basics of creating nodes and tile maps. I don't want to repeat too much of this. If you're having trouble, check out the example project code and refer to the previous chapters.

We need to identify the atlas coordinates of each of the block types we care about and store them in Constants. While we're at it, we should move the levels' blocks enum too:

This is from nodes/globals/constants.gd

```
enum blocks {
    wall_top_left,
    wall_top,
    wall_top_right,
    wall_right,
    wall_bottom_right,
    wall_bottom,
    wall_bottom_left,
    wall_left,
    empty,
    player,
    crate,
    dot,
    door,
}
const _wall_coordinates := Vector2i(8, 7)
const _door_coordinates := Vector2i(10, 0)

const tile_coordinates := {
    blocks.wall_top_left: _wall_coordinates,
    blocks.wall_top: _wall_coordinates,
    blocks.wall_top_right: _wall_coordinates,
    blocks.wall_right: _wall_coordinates,
    blocks.wall_bottom_right: _wall_coordinates,
    blocks.wall_bottom: _wall_coordinates,
    blocks.wall_bottom_left: _wall_coordinates,
    blocks.wall_left: _wall_coordinates,
    blocks.door: _door_coordinates,
}
```

This means our custom GameLevel resource must also change:

This is from resources/levels/level.gd

```
extends Resource
class_name GameLevel

@export var name := "New level"

@export var width := 7

@export var layout : Array[Types.blocks] = [
    Types.blocks.wall_top_left, Types.blocks.wall_top, Types.blocks.wall_
top, Types.blocks.wall_top, Types.blocks.wall_top, Types.blocks.wall_top,
Types.blocks.wall_top_right,
    Types.blocks.wall_left, Types.blocks.empty, Types.blocks.empty, Types.
blocks.empty, Types.blocks.empty, Types.blocks.empty, Types.blocks.
wall_right,
    Types.blocks.wall_left, Types.blocks.empty, Types.blocks.empty, Types.
blocks.empty, Types.blocks.empty, Types.blocks.empty, Types.blocks.
wall_right,
    Types.blocks.wall_left, Types.blocks.empty, Types.blocks.empty, Types.
blocks.empty, Types.blocks.empty, Types.blocks.empty, Types.blocks.
wall_right,
    Types.blocks.wall_left, Types.blocks.empty, Types.blocks.empty, Types.
blocks.empty, Types.blocks.empty, Types.blocks.empty, Types.blocks.
wall_right,
    Types.blocks.wall_left, Types.blocks.empty, Types.blocks.empty, Types.
blocks.empty, Types.blocks.empty, Types.blocks.empty, Types.blocks.
wall_right,
    Types.blocks.wall_bottom_left, Types.blocks.wall_bottom, Types.blocks.
wall_bottom, Types.blocks.wall_bottom, Types.blocks.wall_bottom, Types.
blocks.wall_bottom, Types.blocks.wall_bottom_right,
]
```

You could delete the example array if you're not keen on maintaining this long list of block types. I like to keep these examples around so that it's easier to figure out how to code for the resource.

You might be wondering why I have so many block types when I'm using the same sprite for all of them. It would be simpler to have a single wall type, but that would be less flexible. We could have used any number of tile sets that had different sides and corners of walls; and this enum would account for them all. You're free to simplify the code if the tile set you use doesn't have this level of detail.

We can use these new constants and atlas positions to set the blocks of our tile map on the play screen:

This is from nodes/screens/play_screen.gd

```
extends GameScreen

@onready var _tiles := $Center/Stage/Tiles as TileMap

func _ready() -> void:
    var i := 0
    var level : GameLevel = Variables.current_level
    var half = floor(level.width / 2)
    var remainder = level.width % 2

    for y in range(-half - remainder, half):
        for x in range(-half - remainder, half):
            if Types.tile_coordinates.has(level.layout[i]):
                _tiles.set_cell(0, Vector2i(x, y), 0, Types.tile_
                coordinates[level.layout[i]])

            i += 1
```

This is a strange loop we're using. The tile map's 0,0 coordinate is in the center of the screen; so we want to set blocks on either side of it. If we started at 0,0, then the top-left corner of each level would be in the center of the screen:

Drawing blocks to the left and top of 0,0

Drawing Nodes

Next, we need to create the various level nodes and draw them on the play screen:

1. The player → CharacterBody2D

2. The crates → CharacterBody2D

3. The dots → Area2D

4. The doors → Area2D

Create each of these, with their own attached scripts, until your files look like this:

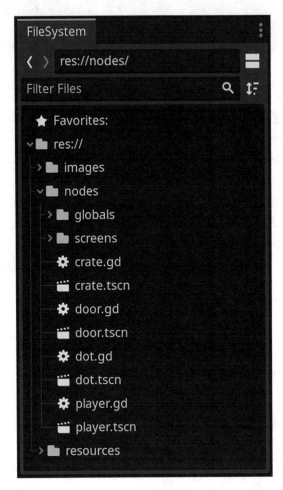

Level nodes

The sprite sheet we've been using to draw walls has visual indicators for all these. I've given the scenes a CollisionShape2D and (except for the door node) a Sprite2D chosen from the sprite sheet. Taking sprites from a sprite sheet can be tricky if you've never done it before. Here are the steps I usually follow:

1. Create the Sprite2D node

2. Set *Texture* ➤ *AtlasTexture*

3. Click *Edit Region*

4. Change *Snap Mode* to *Grid Snap*

5. Change the *Step* values to the size of the sprite (64 × 64 pixels in this case)

6. Select the sprite

Selecting sprites from an `AtlasTexture`

The top-left corner of the sprites and collision shapes should be at 32 × 32 pixels so that their top-left corners align with the top-left corner of each floor square. I've given the scenes custom class names, so we can type-hint against them later on. For now, we need to add them to `Constants`:

This is from `nodes/globals/constants.gd`

```
@export var crate_scene : PackedScene
@export var door_scene : PackedScene
@export var dot_scene : PackedScene
@export var player_scene : PackedScene

@onready var node_scenes := {
    blocks.crate: crate_scene,
    blocks.door: door_scene,
```

```
    blocks.dot: dot_scene,
    blocks.player: player_scene,
}
```

Link these scenes in the property inspector so that we can use them in the play screen code:

This is from nodes/screens/play_screen.gd

```
extends GameScreen

@onready var _tiles := $Center/Stage/Tiles as TileMap
@onready var _nodes := $Center/Stage/Nodes as Node2D

func _ready() -> void:
    var i := 0
    var level : GameLevel = Variables.current_level
    var half = floor(level.width / 2)
    var remainder = level.width % 2

    for y in range(-half - remainder, half):
        for x in range(-half - remainder, half):
            if Types.tile_coordinates.has(level.layout[i]):
                _tiles.set_cell(0, Vector2i(x, y), 0, Types.tile_
                coordinates[level.layout[i]])

            if Constants.node_scenes.has(level.layout[i]):
                var new_node = Constants.node_scenes[level.layout[i]].
                instantiate()
                _nodes.add_child(new_node)
                new_node.position = Vector2(x * 64, y * 64)

            i += 1
```

This new code is similar to the tile map code in terms of how we get the correct data for the type of block. The differences are to do with us creating nodes instead of drawing on a tile map.

We already have x = -4 → 2 and y = -4 → 2; so we can multiply that by the block size to get the top-left position for each node. We could put this pixel size in Constants, but we're already hard-coding the 64 × 64 size by what we've selected as the tile map block size. We'd need to dynamically construct the tile map's source if we wanted it to be completely dynamic.

I don't think it's worth the hassle.

If you find yourself repeating a lot of magic numbers, consider making them constants.

Your levels should now contain any node blocks you've specified in their layout:

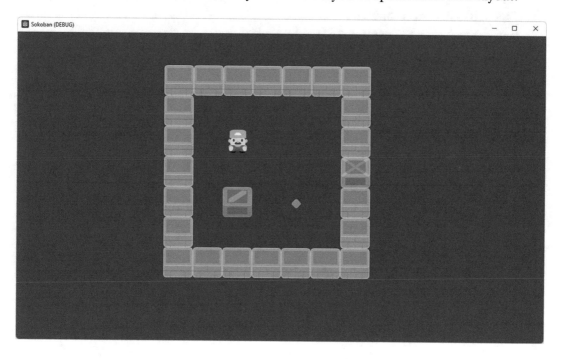

Tiles and nodes in one of my levels

Moving the Player

It's time to add some interactivity! We're going to add some code to listen for player input and move the player... assuming they aren't trying to walk into a wall:

This is from nodes/player.gd

```
extends CharacterBody2D
class_name GamePlayer

@onready var level : GameLevel = Variables.current_level

var walls_blocks := [
    Types.blocks.wall_top_left,
    Types.blocks.wall_top,
    Types.blocks.wall_top_right,
    Types.blocks.wall_right,
    Types.blocks.wall_bottom_right,
    Types.blocks.wall_bottom,
    Types.blocks.wall_bottom_left,
    Types.blocks.wall_left,
]

func _unhandled_key_input(event: InputEvent) -> void:
    if event.is_pressed():
        var offset = Vector2(0, 0)

        if event.is_action_pressed("ui_right"):
            offset.x = 64
        if event.is_action_pressed("ui_down"):
            offset.y = 64
        if event.is_action_pressed("ui_left"):
            offset.x = -64
        if event.is_action_pressed("ui_up"):
            offset.y = -64

        var target_block = block_at_position(position + offset)

        if not walls_blocks.has(target_block):
            position = position + offset

func block_at_position(position : Vector2) -> int:
    var i := 0
    var half = floor(level.width / 2)
    var remainder = level.width % 2
```

```
for y in range(-half - remainder, half):
    for x in range(-half - remainder, half):
        if position.x == x * 64 and position.y == y * 64:
            return level.layout[i]

        i += 1

return -1
```

A great way to listen for keyboard input is to add an _unhandled_key_input method to our player class. In our recreation of Sokoban, a single press of the left key means the player tries to move 64 pixels to the left.

Thus, we change the offset (which is a change to the player's position) depending on which of the ui_* keys the player presses. We figure out if there's a wall in the new position using a form of the same strange loops we used before in drawing.

If there's no wall, we add the offset position to the player's current position.

Now is a good time to relaunch the game to see if pressing the arrow keys on your keyboard will move the player. Even if you can move, there are some strange things you'll notice.

You can walk through a crate, dot, and door without restriction. You'll even walk underneath the crate and dot if the player appears above them in the node tree.

Avoiding Closed Doors

The player should not be able to leave through the door until all crates are on dots. Let's add a check for this. First, we need to remember how many crates there are in a level's layout and how many are covered by crates:

This is from nodes/globals/variables.gd

```
var total_crates : int
var covered_crates : int
```

We can reset and increment these when we draw a level layout on the play screen:

This is from nodes/screens/play_screen.gd

```
Variables.total_crates = 0
Variables.covered_crates = 0
```

```
for y in range(-half - remainder, half):
    for x in range(-half - remainder, half):
        if Types.tile_coordinates.has(level.layout[i]):
            # ...snip

        if Constants.node_scenes.has(level.layout[i]):
            # ...snip

        if level.layout[i] == Types.blocks.crate:
            Variables.total_crates += 1

        i += 1
```

Using these (and a bit of refactoring), we can prevent a player from leaving through a closed door:

This is from nodes/player.gd

```
var is_wall : bool = walls_blocks.has(target_block)
var is_closed_door : bool = target_block == Types.blocks.door and
Variables.covered_crates < Variables.total_crates

if not is_wall and not is_closed_door:
    position = position + offset
```

Moving Crates

The last bit of movement we need to add is the ability to move crates. This is an extension of wall checking on the player. If the player is next to a crate and moves in the direction of the crate and there is space to move the crate....

This is from nodes/player.gd

```
func _unhandled_key_input(event: InputEvent) -> void:
    if event.is_pressed():
        var offset = Vector2(0, 0)

        if event.is_action_pressed("ui_right"):
            offset.x = 64
        if event.is_action_pressed("ui_down"):
```

```
        offset.y = 64
    if event.is_action_pressed("ui_left"):
        offset.x = -64
    if event.is_action_pressed("ui_up"):
        offset.y = -64

    var target_block := block_at_position(position + offset)
    var further_target_block := block_at_position(position + offset
    + offset)

    var is_wall : bool = walls_blocks.has(target_block)
    var is_closed_door : bool = target_block == Types.blocks.door and
    Variables.covered_crates < Variables.total_crates

    var crate := crate_at_position(position + offset)
    var is_crate_blocked_by_wall : bool = walls_blocks.has(further_
    target_block)

    if crate and not is_crate_blocked_by_wall:
        crate.position = crate.position + offset
        position = position + offset
    elif not crate and not is_wall and not is_closed_door:
        position = position + offset
func crate_at_position(position: Vector2) -> GameCrate:
    for child in get_parent().get_children():
        if child is GameCrate and child.position.x == position.x and child.
        position.y == position.y:
            return child
    return null
```

We start by checking the space we want the player to move into **and** the space beyond it. That's because the player might be trying to move into a space occupied by a crate; and we'd want to know if the crate can move.

The player movement code now needs to account for

1. If the player is trying to push a crate

2. ...and there's enough space for the crate to be pushed by the player

or

1. If the player is not trying to push a crate

2. ...or trying to walk into a wall

3. ...or trying to walk through a closed door

Relaunch the game and try this movement code out. It's pretty cool. Unfortunately, we still have the issue of the player and crate disappearing behind dots if the player and crate are above the dots in the node tree.

The simplest way to sort this out is to go to the *Node2D* properties (of the crate and player) and make the *Z Index* values greater than those of the dot:

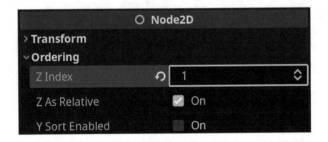

Higher Z Index value means closer to the screen.

Winning a Level

All that remains is to show that the player has covered all the dots with crates by allowing the player to leave.

First, we need to connect to signals on the dots:

Connecting to the body events on dots

The best events for this are on_body_entered and on_body_existed. These are emitted when a CharacterBody2D or StaticBody2D collides with this Area2D. This is what that code looks like:

This is from nodes/dot.gd

```
extends Area2D
class_name GameDot

func _on_dot_body_entered(body) -> void:
    if body is GameCrate:
        Variables.covered_crates += 1

func _on_dot_body_exited(body) -> void:
    if body is GameCrate:
        Variables.covered_crates -= 1
```

There are two bodies that could collide with each dot – a player or a crate. So we need to make sure that we only add to the covered crate count when the body that is colliding is a crate.

Before these collisions will work, we need to set up collision layers and assign the dots and crates to them:

Defining new collision layers

We assign these layers through the property inspector:

Assigning nodes to collision layers

Set the following things:

1. In Crate, set *Layer* to crates.

2. In Crate, set *Mask* to dots.

3. In Dot, set *Layer* to dots.

4. In Dot, set *Mask* to crates.

Layers and masks can be tricky to understand. *Layer* is "what layers this collider is in," and *Mask* is "what layers this collider will collide with." After the preceding changes, crates will collide with dots and vice versa. We only need one side of that for our code to work, but I like to set both sides up unless there's a good reason not to.

To test this, relaunch the game and move the crate over the top of the dot. You should now be able to walk through the door. We can take this a step further by connecting to the on_body_entered signal:

Listening for door events

Now, we can respond to the player moving through the open doorway:

This is from nodes/door.gd

```
extends Area2D
class_name GameDoor

func _on_door_body_entered(body) -> void:
    if body is GamePlayer:
        body.queue_free()
        print("You win!")
```

If the player leaves through the open door, we remove their avatar from the level and print a console message. It's not the most flashy ending; but it's a starting point for anything more elaborate you'd like to do with it.

One thing I noticed was that using collision shapes that are exactly 64 × 64 pixels would cause the player to collide with the door even when they are in the block next to the door. This meant the player would exit the stage even when the player's code prevented them from entering the door's space. I adjusted all my collision shapes to be 60 × 60 pixels big and to start at 30 × 30 pixels; so there's always four pixels of space between the collision shapes.

Summary

This has been a whirlwind of a chapter. We've used all the skills gained so far to build out a real game. It might need a bit of polish, but you're welcome to do that so that you can release it as a game of your own.

Take a bit of time to review the mechanics you built for this game. Swap the sprites and tiles out for your own art, or a different art pack from kenny.nl. Add a more flashy win message, with particles and overlays and everything. This is a time for you to be creative and excited about what you have achieved.

CHAPTER 5

Designing Levels in Pixel Art

Our Sokoban implementation is pretty cool, but it has a problem that I'd like to solve in this chapter. We could keep designing our levels with Godot's visual tools, but there's a better way to handle procedural content.

In fact, we started down the better path while designing our levels in Sokoban. You might have wondered why we used an obscure grid system when we could draw levels by hand.

It's because algorithms can use grid-based data like this to render our tiles and nodes for us. All we have to do is find an easier way to define the grid data.

Creating Pixel Art

Creating any kind of art has its challenges, so I won't pretend to give you shortcuts for it. All I know is that pixel art offers a set of constraints (limit color palette and canvas size) that encourage creativity in me.

There are a bunch of applications you can use to draw pixel art. If you want something free, you can try Piskel. I can also recommend Aseprite, though it's not free.

Try either, and create a bit of pixel art that is 16 × 16 pixels:

© Christopher Pitt 2023
C. Pitt, *Procedural Generation in Godot*, https://doi.org/10.1007/978-1-4842-8795-8_5

Example pixel layout

What we want to do is try to represent a typical game level in pixel art so that we can parse that image file inside of Godot. In this example:

- Green pixels represent trees.

- Gray ones represent rocks.

- The orange pixel represents the player.

You don't have to use the same colors or layout. You'll soon see how to accommodate different designs and colors.

Converting Pixel Art to a Grid

Let's open up our experiment project and add a new one for this pixel art code. Import the pixel art image you created and set up a new inherited scene, from the Experiment scene, called PixelsExperiment:

Setting the stage

Pixel art is a grid, by design. We need to use some new code to get the grid data out of the image and into a format that we can manipulate and draw.

Let's add some methods to do this in PixelsExperiment:

This is from nodes/experiments/pixels_experiment.gd

```
extends GameExperiment

@export var layout_texture : Texture2D

enum types {
    none,
    tree,
```

```
    rock,
    player,
}

const type_colors := {
    types.tree: "65a30d",
    types.rock: "57534e",
    types.player: "ea580c",
}

func _ready() -> void:
    var layout = get_layout()
    # ...do something with the layout

func get_layout() -> Array[Array]:
    var layout_image := layout_texture.get_image()
    var rows := []

    for y in layout_texture.get_height():
        var row := []

        for x in layout_texture.get_width():
            var type := types.none
            var color := layout_image.get_pixel(x, y).to_html(false)

            for t in types.values():
                if not type_colors.has(t):
                    continue

                if color == type_colors[t]:
                    type = t

            row.append(type)
        rows.append(row)

    return rows
```

As you can probably tell, I created an enum of the possible types of pixels I have in my image file. I care about the three colors: for trees, rocks, and the player.

I use the enum values as keys for a dictionary that holds the hexadecimal colors of each type. This creates a type-safe lookup for the colors while also being quick to extend with more colors.

We export a Texture2D because it allows for any popular image format to be set through the property inspector. It has a get_image method we can use to get the underlying image data.

This Image class has a get_pixel method, which is what we can use to get the image grid's pixel data to inspection. get_pixel returns a Color instance, which we can convert to a hexadecimal value.

We can compare the dictionary of colors to the pixel color to figure out what the type of each pixel. This gives us a similar grid to the one we built in Sokoban.

Flipping Layouts

Here's where things get more interesting. We can take this pixel grid data and manipulate it to create variation. Let's start by flipping the grid:

This is from nodes/experiments/pixels_experiment.gd

```
enum flip_axis {
    none,
    x,
    y,
}
func flip_layout(layout: Array[Array], flip := flip_axis.none) ->
Array[Array]:
    var new_rows := []

    for row in layout:
        var new_row := []

        for cell in row:
            if flip == flip_axis.x:
                new_row.push_front(cell)
            else:
                new_row.push_back(cell)
```

```
        if flip == flip_axis.y:
            new_rows.push_front(new_row)
        else:
            new_rows.push_back(new_row)

    return new_rows
```

Since we have the pixels in a multidimensional array, flipping is a matter of reversing the direction of rows or cells in each row. We can make use of this by passing the layout through this new method:

This is from nodes/experiments/pixels-experiment.gd

```
func _ready() -> void:
    var layout = get_layout()
    var flipped_layout = flip_layout(layout, flip_axis.y)

    # ...do something with the flipped_layout
```

This is one of many different manipulations possible with this kind of grid data structure. In a couple chapters, we'll see how useful it can be for generating varied maps.

Combining with Nodes and Tile Maps

We can combine this knowledge with what we learned in the Sokoban project. We can use this array in place of one that we built by hand:

```
for row in layout:
    for cell in row:
        if tiles.has(cell):
            _tiles.set_cell(
                0, Vector2i(x, y), 0, tiles[cell]
            )

        if nodes.has(cell):
            var new_node = nodes[cell].instantiate()
            _nodes.add_child(new_node)
            new_node.position = Vector2(x * 64, y * 64)
```

Summary

In this chapter, we took our first steps toward designing our levels with pixel art. While converting images to arrays isn't groundbreaking, we can manipulate those arrays in interesting ways.

Take a bit of time to think of other kinds of manipulations we could do to the resulting pixel art grids. Can you think of how to rotate a layout, or how we could vary the drawing of cells to inject a bit of realism and randomness?

In the next chapter, we're going to dive even deeper into the randomness aspect of content generation, as we gear up to build our next game.

CHAPTER 6

Creating a Seeding System

Back in Chapter 2, we learned that randomization takes a couple forms in game development. The first and most common is randomization where we don't explicitly control the seed used. That's what we used to randomize the behavior of the nodes in that chapter.

The second form of randomization is where we know what the seed is, and we can control it to some extent. Minecraft is a great example of this, because each level starts with an input where you can specify a seed.

Seeding can be a bit confusing, but it's a way to start the randomization algorithm at an unguessable point. That's because most randomization isn't true randomization but rather pseudo-randomization.

Computers cannot produce random numbers without observing some outside stimulus; so instead, they offer a predictable kind of randomization progression.

Imagine an infinite sequence of random numbers. Seeding is a way to start at some point in the sequence and continue it:

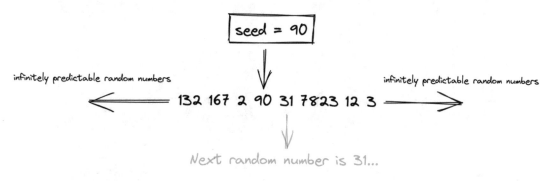

Seeded randomization

© Christopher Pitt 2023
C. Pitt, *Procedural Generation in Godot*, https://doi.org/10.1007/978-1-4842-8795-8_6

If we pick a different seed, then the starting point is different, so the sequence of random numbers will be different. If someone using the same algorithm picks the seed of 90, they will get the same sequence of numbers.

Minecraft picks a random seed, seeded from details like the date and time and details of the computer's hardware and configuration.

That seed is then used as the starting point for the pseudo-random number generation to create what appears to be a completely random world.

A New Experiment

We'll become more familiar with these concepts as we see them in action. Let's create a new experiment where we study the effects of pseudo-randomization and create a way for starting seeds to be derived and changed.

Let's call it the SeedExperiment. We can add the following component tree, so we can edit the seed value and see a sample of random numbers that are generated with that seed:

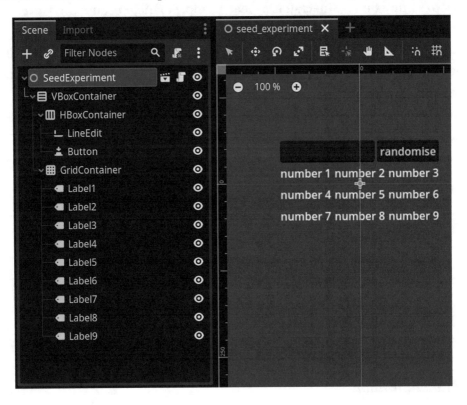

Setting up SeedExperiment

You can make these UI controls as small or as big as you like. We can't anchor them to the screen because their parent is a Node2D, so it has no implicit size. We can set up a couple methods to pick a new random number and to update the sample of random numbers (the labels):

This is from nodes/experiments/seed_experiment.gd

```
extends GameExperiment

@onready var _line_edit := $VBoxContainer/HBoxContainer/LineEdit as LineEdit
@onready var _grid_container := $VBoxContainer/GridContainer as
GridContainer

func pick_random_number() -> void:
    _line_edit.text = str(randi() % 100)

func update_random_sample() -> void:
    var generator = RandomNumberGenerator.new()
    generator.seed = _line_edit.text.to_int()

    for child in _grid_container.get_children():
        child.text = str(generator.randi() % 100)
```

Here, we can see both popular forms of randomization. The first is in pick_random_number, where we're not defining a seed to start from. When the game starts, the randomize() function is automatically called. This is much the same way as Minecraft does to generate the seed, which it then allows the player to edit.

The second kind of randomization happens in update_random_sample, where we define the seed for the RandomNumberGenerator so that it starts at a predictable point.

We can tie these methods together by adding some signals to the LineEdit and Button, and we can also make the randomization process happen once on load:

This is from nodes/experiments/seed_experiment.gd

```
func _ready() -> void:
    refresh()

func refresh() -> void:
    pick_random_number()
    update_random_sample()
```

```
func _on_button_pressed() -> void:
    refresh()

func _on_line_edit_text_changed(_new_text: String) -> void:
    update_random_sample()
```

When the experiment starts, it will update the LineEdit with a random number between 0 and 99. This is used to update all the labels to use this as the seed.

Press the *randomize* button a few times to see the different samples. Then, edit the value of the LineEdit so that you switch back and forth between two known seeds. You'll see that each time you put in the same seed number, the same sample set of random numbers appears.

That's the power of seeded randomization. You can share the same experiences with your friends, even in a random system, if they use the same seed as you.

Generating Easier Seeds

A random number or sequence of random characters is difficult to remember. Random number generators tend to use longer seeds so that the seed is harder to guess.

Why force your players to remember a sequence of numbers when you can show them with something much easier, like two or three words? Those are much easier to memorize.

Search on Google or GitHub for a word list file in text format. I'm using one that is about 23KB big. I forget where exactly I found it, but I used it for a game I made a couple years ago.

Once you've found one, put it into the experiment project so that we can load it into this experiment. Then, we can use code like this to load all the words and allow us to select the desired number of words for our seed:

Downloading a words file

This is from nodes/experiments/seed_experiment.gd

```
func get_words(generator : RandomNumberGenerator, number : int = 3) ->
PackedStringArray:
    var words := get_all_words()
    var size := words.size()

    var chosen := []

    for i in range(3):
        chosen.append(words[generator.randi() % size])

    return PackedStringArray(chosen)

func get_all_words() -> PackedStringArray:
    var file = File.new()

    if file.file_exists("res://resources/objects.txt"):
        file.open("res://resources/objects.txt", File.READ)
        var content = file.get_as_text()
```

```
        file.close()
        return content.split("\n", false)

    return PackedStringArray()
```

The RandomNumberGenerator's seed property must be an integer, which we can get using the hash method on strings:

This is from nodes/experiments/seed_experiment.gd

```
func get_hash_from_words(words : PackedStringArray) -> int:
    var complete = ""

    for word in words:
        complete += word.trim_prefix(" ").trim_suffix(" ").to_lower()

    return complete.hash()
```

Now, all we need to do is replace the numeric seeds we were generating with these new methods:

This is from nodes/experiments/seed_experiment.gd

```
var generator : RandomNumberGenerator

func pick_random_words() -> void:
    _line_edit.text = " ".join(get_words(generator))

func update_random_sample() -> void:
    generator.seed = get_hash_from_words(_line_edit.text.split(" "))

    for child in _grid_container.get_children():
        child.text = str(generator.randi() % 100)

func _ready() -> void:
    generator = RandomNumberGenerator.new()
    refresh()

func refresh() -> void:
    pick_random_words()
    update_random_sample()
```

It seems a bit silly that we're getting a PackedStringArray of words from get_all_words, getting a PackedStringArray from get_words, joining them together, and splitting them into another PackedStringArray to get the hash. It's because we want to show the words to the user, and LineEdit's text property can only be a string.

This makes the seeds a lot easier to remember and share, because it's a small number of words to remember.

The hash method's documentation is careful to point out that identical strings can generate identical hashes to each other, but that the reverse isn't always true. The hash value is a 32-bit integer, which means larger values are limited to 32-bit representations. Different values can generate identical hashes, because of that loss of specificity. This is called a collision, and it's common to talk about the possibility of collisions in cryptography.

In fact, seeded randomization has many of the same underpinnings as encryption. Reversible encryption values are only as strong as the encryption algorithm and the secrecy of the key used to seed them. Sound familiar? If someone knows the randomization algorithm and seed, they can reproduce the same sequence of random values.

Summary

In this chapter, we learned all about generating seeds so that we can control the randomization that can occur in our games. We're going to use this knowledge in the next chapter, as we build a new game.

Take some time to think about how to integrate this code into a larger project. How would you structure this code if it wasn't on the "play" screen? How can you call into it to get the words and use them to randomize the behavior of worlds and NPCs?

CHAPTER 7

Recreating Bouncy Cars

It's time for us to use everything we've learned so far to recreate another game. This time, it's a game that I made a few years ago, called Bouncy Cars.

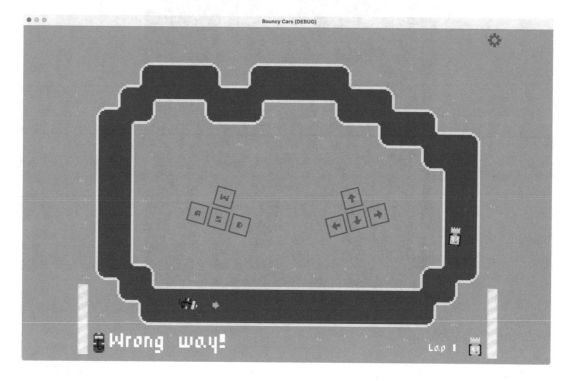

Bouncy Cars (2021)

Bouncy Cars is a local coop racing game where each course is procedurally generated. The aim of the game is to complete five laps without blowing up. Players can take damage if they collide with the race-way barriers or each other.

It's the sixth game I made, yet it's still one of the most polished I released. It includes robust procedural generation algorithm that makes each course unique and error-free.

© Christopher Pitt 2023
C. Pitt, *Procedural Generation in Godot*, https://doi.org/10.1007/978-1-4842-8795-8_7

Getting Set Up

Let's get started by creating a new project. We want all the usual things, like a base Screen node inherited by menu and play screens.

Creating screen nodes

We also need a base CharacterBody2D which our different vehicles can inherit from. We can create their default behavior and then customize each vehicle.

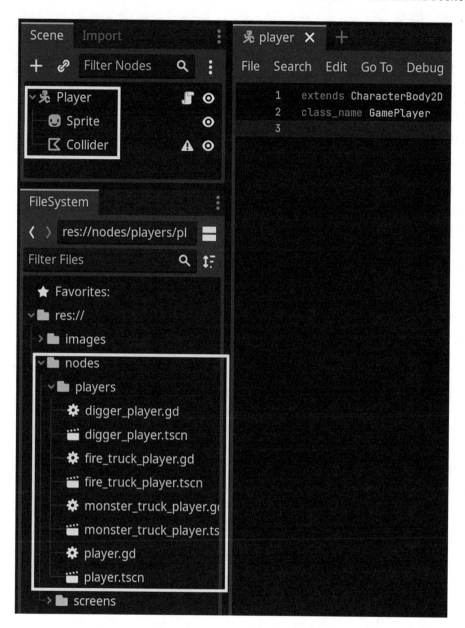

Creating player nodes

We need a way to switch between screens, like we did in Chapter 4. For this, create a global Screens node and set it to autoload. We can use similar code to that of Chapter 4 to switch between different scenes:

This is from nodes/globals/screens.gd

```
extends Node

var root = null
var current_screen : Types.screens
var current_screen_node : GameScreen
var is_changing_screen := false

func _ready() -> void:
    root = get_tree().get_root()
    current_screen_node = root.get_children().back()

func change_screen(new_screen: Types.screens) -> void:
    if is_changing_screen:
        return

    is_changing_screen = true

    var new_screen_node : GameScreen = Constants.screen_scenes[new_screen].
    instantiate()
    load_new_screen(new_screen_node, new_screen)

func load_new_screen(new_screen_node: GameScreen, new_screen: Types.
screens) -> void:
    current_screen_node.queue_free()
    root.add_child(new_screen_node)

    current_screen = new_screen
    current_screen_node = new_screen_node

    is_changing_screen = false
```

We can define the various screen references in a Constants global:

This is from nodes/globals/constants.gd

```
extends Node
class_name Types

enum screens {
    none,
```

```
    menu,
    new_game,
    play,
}

@export var menu_scene: PackedScene
@export var new_game_scene: PackedScene
@export var play_scene: PackedScene

@onready var screen_scenes := {
    screens.menu: menu_scene,
    screens.new_game: new_game_scene,
    screens.play: play_scene,
}
```

Now, we can add a few buttons to the screen nodes we've made so that we can switch back and forth between them. I'll show you what this looks like for the main menu, and you can extrapolate from there for the remaining screens.

Main menu nodes

We've got the usual arrangement of `CenterContainer`, `VBoxContainer`, and `Button` nodes. This places three buttons in a vertical alignment in the center of the screen. We can attach listeners to these buttons so that screens change when we press a button:

This is from nodes/screens/main_menu_screen.gd

```
extends GameScreen
```

```
func _on_new_game_pressed() -> void:
    Screens.change_screen(Constants.screens.new_game)
```

```
func _on_quit_pressed() -> void:
    get_tree().quit()
```

Not all platforms have this notion of quitting something. That's very much a desktop PC thing. It would be cool if we can hide the quit button on platforms where someone can press a home button or close a tab:

This is from nodes/screens/main_menu_screen.gd

```
@onready var _quit := $Center/Buttons/Quit
```

```
func _ready() -> void:
    if OS.has_feature("HTML5") or OS.get_name() == "iOS" or OS.get_name()
    == "Android":
        _quit.visible = false
```

Don't forget, we need to configure the window size as we did before:

- Changing the viewport size to 320 × 240

- Changing the window override size to 1280 × 960

- Changing the *Stretch* ➤ *Mode* to canvas_items

- Changing the *Stretch* ➤ *Aspect* to expand

This will expand and center the interface, giving full weight to the pixel art.

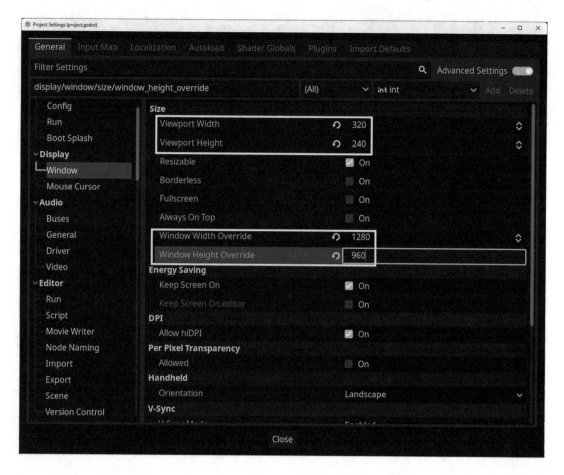

Changing window size

Changing stretch settings

Creating a Seed Screen

We're going to use some of the seed-based generation we learned about in the previous chapter. When selecting *New Game*, we'll present players with a screen that shows them a random seed phrase. They can choose to keep or customize this phrase.

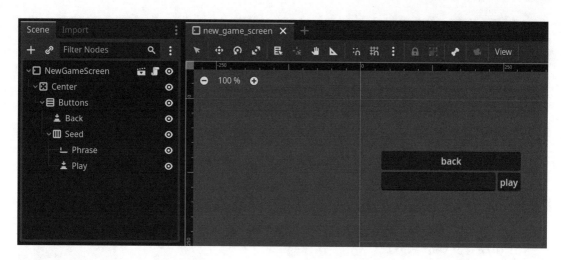

New Game screen

I expanded the width of the LineEdit to 200 pixels.

Let's copy some of the code we created in the previous chapter, to select three words for our seed. We also need the text file of words we downloaded for this purpose:

This is from nodes/globals/generation.gd

```
extends Node

@export_file("*.txt") var words_file

var generator : RandomNumberGenerator

func _ready() -> void:
    generator = RandomNumberGenerator.new()
    generator.randomize()

func get_three_words_phrase() -> String:
    return " ".join(get_words(generator))

func get_words(generator : RandomNumberGenerator, number : int = 3) ->
PackedStringArray:
    var words := get_all_words()
    var size := words.size()

    var chosen := []
```

```
    for i in range(3):
        chosen.append(words[generator.randi() % size])

    return PackedStringArray(chosen)

func get_all_words() -> PackedStringArray:
    var file = File.new()
    file.open(words_file, File.READ)

    var content = file.get_as_text()

    file.close()

    return content.split("\n", false)

func get_hash_from_words(words : PackedStringArray) -> int:
    var complete = ""

    for word in words:
        complete += word.trim_prefix(" ").trim_suffix(" ").to_lower()

    return complete.hash()
```

Exporting file variables with extension filter

This is like the experiment, but we're now exporting the file reference instead of hard-coding the file path. This means we can move the file or global without the link between the two breaking. It also means we no longer have to check for the presence of the file before reading from it.

Remember to autoload the Generation node.

We can use this in the NewGame screen to populate the phrase input:

This is from nodes/screens/new_game_screen.gd

```
@onready var _phrase := $Center/Items/Seed/Phrase as LineEdit

func _on_back_pressed() -> void:
    Screens.change_screen(Types.screens.main_menu)

func _ready() -> void:
    _phrase.text = Generation.get_three_words_phrase()
```

This means the Phrase node will have a random phrase in it as soon as the NewGame screen loads. It is an editable control because we have to allow for the possibility that the user will change the seed.

Generating Maps

The question now is what to do with this seed phrase. One simple way to generate random maps is to create a set of "corners" that can be randomly selected and algorithmically modified. Here's an example of what I mean:

Corner samples

Each of these corners is a potential layout for a quarter of the race track. To select from them, we need a method that can read the image data and convert it to a multidimensional array of cell or tile types. Let's start with some constants for cell types and pixel colors:

This is from nodes/globals/constants.gd

```
enum cells {
    none,
    grass,
    road,
```

```
    player_1_start,
    player_2_start,
    waypoint,
}

const cell_colors := {
    cells.grass: "38a169",
    cells.road: "4a5568",
    cells.player_1_start: "f687b3",
    cells.player_2_start: "f6ad55",
    cells.waypoint: "4fd1c5",
}

const segment_width := 10
const segment_height := 7

enum segment_types {
    top_left,
    top_right,
    bottom_left,
    bottom_right,
}

const number_of_segments := 6
```

We can use pixel data to get a multidimensional array of cell types:

This is from nodes/globals/generation.gd

```
func get_deep_corner_array(image: Image, offset_segment: int) -> Array:
    var rows = []

    for y in Constants.segment_height:
        var row = []

        for x in Constants.segment_width:
            var cell = Types.cells.none

            match image.get_pixel(x + (offset_segment * Constants.segment_
            width), y).to_html(false):
```

```
            Types.cell_colors[Types.cells.grass]:
                cell = Types.cells.grass
            Types.cell_colors[Types.cells.road]:
                cell = Types.cells.road
            Types.cell_colors[Types.cells.player_1_start]:
                cell = Types.cells.player_1_start
            Types.cell_colors[Types.cells.player_2_start]:
                cell = Types.cells.player_2_start
            Types.cell_colors[Types.cells.waypoint]:
                cell = Types.cells.waypoint

        row.push_back(cell)

    rows.push_back(row)

  return rows
```

Since the corners image is a single row of corner designs, we can use an integer offset to fetch the pixel data for a complete corner. An offset of 1 means going a full segment_ width (or, in this case, 10 pixels) to the right.

The rest of the code is straight out of Chapter 5, albeit with different cell types and colors. Feel free to go back to that chapter to brush up on this approach if you need to.

We can start to build up a complete race course map by fetching all the corners and picking a clockwise or anticlockwise direction:

This is from nodes/globals/generation.gd

```
@export var layout_texture : Texture2D

func get_map(user_three_words_phrase = null) -> Dictionary:
    var three_words = null

    if typeof(user_three_words_phrase) == TYPE_STRING:
        three_words = user_three_words_phrase.split(" ")
    else:
        three_words = get_three_words_phrase().split(" ")

    generator.seed = get_hash_from_words(three_words)

    var clockwise = generator.randi() & 1
```

```
var top_left_offset = generator.randi() % Constants.number_of_segments
var top_right_offset = generator.randi() % Constants.number_of_segments
var bottom_left_offset = generator.randi() % Constants.number_of_
segments
var bottom_right_offset = generator.randi() % Constants.number_of_
segments

var segments_image = layout_texture.get_image()

var top_left_deep_corner = get_deep_corner_array(segments_image, top_
left_offset)
var top_right_deep_corner = get_deep_corner_array(segments_image, top_
right_offset)
var bottom_left_deep_corner = get_deep_corner_array(segments_image,
bottom_left_offset)
var bottom_right_deep_corner = get_deep_corner_array(segments_image,
bottom_right_offset)

return {
    "three_words": three_words,
    "clockwise": clockwise,
    # ...
}
```

If we were to call this method and print the results, we'd see four arrays of cell types, all randomly selected. That's a great start, but we need a way to create a loop from what would otherwise be four top-left corners.

Let's add a method to flip the corners using code like what we had a couple chapters ago:

This is from nodes/globals/generation.gd

```
func get_flipped_corner_array(deep_corner_array: Array, should_flip_x: bool
= false, should_flip_y: bool = false) -> Array:
    var new_rows = []

    for row in deep_corner_array:
        var new_row = []
```

```
    for cell in row:
        if should_flip_x:
            new_row.push_front(cell)
        else:
            new_row.push_back(cell)

    if should_flip_y:
        new_rows.push_front(new_row)
    else:
        new_rows.push_back(new_row)

  return new_rows
```

This method can flip vertically or horizontally; so we could turn a "top-left" corner into a "bottom-right" corner by flipping both directions. It's a mirrored rotation.

We can extend our get_map method to flip the corners:

This is from nodes/globals/generation.gd

```
var top_left_flipped_corner = get_flipped_corner_array(top_left_deep_
corner, false, false)
var top_right_flipped_corner = get_flipped_corner_array(top_right_deep_
corner, true, false)
var bottom_left_flipped_corner = get_flipped_corner_array(bottom_left_deep_
corner, false, true)
var bottom_right_flipped_corner = get_flipped_corner_array(bottom_right_
deep_corner, true, true)
```

We need to squash the cells into a simpler array (along with some extra metadata) so that they're easier to draw. You've probably noticed code about "waypoints". There's going to be a bit more now, which we'll go into more detail about in a bit.

This is from nodes/globals/generation.gd

```
func get_shallow_corner_array(deep_corner_array: Array, offset_row: int,
offset_cell: int, segment_type: int) -> Dictionary:
    var cells = []
    var waypoints = []

    var i = 0
```

```
    for row in deep_corner_array.size():
        for cell in deep_corner_array[row].size():
            cells.push_back({
                "y": row + offset_row,
                "x": cell + offset_cell,
                "type": deep_corner_array[row][cell],
            })

            if deep_corner_array[row][cell] == Types.cells.waypoint:
                waypoints.push_back({
                    "y": row + offset_row,
                    "x": cell + offset_cell,
                    "segment_type": segment_type,
                    "index": i,
                })

                i += 1
    return {
        "cells": cells,
        "waypoints": waypoints,
    }
```

This new method takes a multidimensional array and squashes it into two one-dimensional arrays: one for waypoint cells and one for all cells. We're almost ready to start drawing a map, but we still need to finish up the get_map method:

This is from nodes/globals/generation.gd

```
func get_map(user_three_words_phrase = null) -> Dictionary:
    var three_words = null

    if typeof(user_three_words_phrase) == TYPE_STRING:
        three_words = user_three_words_phrase.split(" ")
    else:
        three_words = get_three_words_phrase().split(" ")

    generator.seed = get_hash_from_words(three_words)

    var clockwise = generator.randi() & 1
```

```
var top_left_offset = generator.randi() % Constants.number_of_segments
var top_right_offset = generator.randi() % Constants.number_of_segments
var bottom_left_offset = generator.randi() % Constants.number_of_
segments
var bottom_right_offset = generator.randi() % Constants.number_of_
segments

var segments_image = layout_texture.get_image()

var top_left_deep_corner = get_deep_corner_array(segments_image, top_
left_offset)
var top_right_deep_corner = get_deep_corner_array(segments_image, top_
right_offset)
var bottom_left_deep_corner = get_deep_corner_array(segments_image,
bottom_left_offset)
var bottom_right_deep_corner = get_deep_corner_array(segments_image,
bottom_right_offset)

var top_left_flipped_corner = get_flipped_corner_array(top_left_deep_
corner, false, false)
var top_right_flipped_corner = get_flipped_corner_array(top_right_deep_
corner, true, false)
var bottom_left_flipped_corner = get_flipped_corner_array(bottom_left_
deep_corner, false, true)
var bottom_right_flipped_corner = get_flipped_corner_array(bottom_
right_deep_corner, true, true)

var top_left_shallow_corner = get_shallow_corner_array(top_left_
flipped_corner, 0, 0, Types.segment_types.top_left)
var top_right_shallow_corner = get_shallow_corner_array(top_right_
flipped_corner, 0, Constants.segment_width, Types.segment_types.
top_right)
var bottom_left_shallow_corner = get_shallow_corner_array(bottom_left_
flipped_corner, Constants.segment_height, 0, Types.segment_types.
bottom_left)
var bottom_right_shallow_corner = get_shallow_corner_array(bottom_
right_flipped_corner, Constants.segment_height, Constants.segment_
width, Types.segment_types.bottom_right)
```

111

```
var cells = []
cells += top_left_shallow_corner.cells
cells += top_right_shallow_corner.cells
cells += bottom_left_shallow_corner.cells
cells += bottom_right_shallow_corner.cells

var waypoints = []
waypoints += top_left_shallow_corner.waypoints
waypoints += top_right_shallow_corner.waypoints
waypoints += bottom_left_shallow_corner.waypoints
waypoints += bottom_right_shallow_corner.waypoints

return {
    "cells": cells,
    "waypoints": waypoints,
    "generator": generator,
    "three_words": three_words,
    "clockwise": clockwise,
}
```

Aside from the complete set of cells and waypoints, we also want to return the seed words, the clockwise/anticlockwise direction, and the generator. The seed words could be user-supplied but will usually be random. The generator is useful in case we need to generate anything in the caller that must be based on the same seed.

Drawing the Map

We've finished the code we need to tell Godot what to build, but now we need to write the code to tell Godot how to build it. That means taking these arrays and turning them into tiles and nodes!

We need to store the intended three words (or phrase) that the player has selected. This means creating a new global and interacting with it from the play screen:

This is from nodes/globals/variables.gd

```
extends Node

var current_phrase : String
```

This will store the intended seed phrase so that we can reuse it in generation on later screens.

Remember to autoload the Generation node.

We need to set this when the seed screen is being used:

This is from nodes/screens/new_game_screen.gd

```
func _ready() -> void:
    var phrase = Generation.get_three_words_phrase()
    Variables.current_phrase = phrase
    _phrase.text = phrase

func _on_phrase_text_changed(new_text: String) -> void:
    Variables.current_phrase = _phrase.text

func _on_play_pressed() -> void:
    Screens.change_screen(Types.screens.play)
```

Don't forget to attach the *Play* button's pressed() signal to _on_play_pressed(). We can use the current_phrase variable when we're drawing the map on the Play screen:

This is from nodes/screens/play_screen.gd

```
extends GameScreen

var map : Dictionary

func _ready() -> void:
    reset()

func reset() -> void:
    map = Generation.get_map(Variables.current_phrase)

    draw_map()
    draw_players()

    calculate_waypoints()
```

```
func draw_map() -> void:
    pass

func draw_players() -> void:
    pass

func calculate_waypoints() -> void:
    pass
```

Drawing the map requires doing three distinct passes: static visuals, player nodes, and the waypoint system. We're going to start with the static visuals. We've got the array of cells, so now we need to loop through it and draw each cell based on its type. Add a TileMap node to PlayScreen, called Tiles. We can draw on in the draw_map() function:

This is from nodes/screens/play_screen.gd

```
@onready var _tiles := $Tiles as TileMap

func draw_map() -> void:
    for cell in map.cells:
        var roads : Array[Vector2i] = []

        if [
            Types.cells.road,
            Types.cells.player_1_start,
            Types.cells.player_2_start,
            Types.cells.waypoint
        ].has(cell.type):
            roads.append(Vector2i(cell.x, cell.y))

        _tiles.set_cells_terrain_connect(0, roads, 0, 0, false)
```

The set_cells_terrain_connect method takes an array of nodes to draw, with the desired terrain, and connects them all together using bit masks. It requires that we set up a TileMap and TileSet on PlayScreen, with a road terrain. I'm using this image as my road terrain:

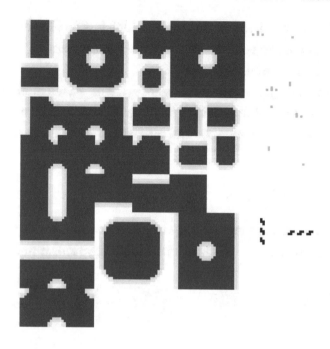

Road tiles

This is the original artwork from Bouncy Cars; but we're not going to use it all in this chapter. The important bits are the gray road sections. Go ahead and set up a terrain with these. Here's what the bit masks look like for my terrain:

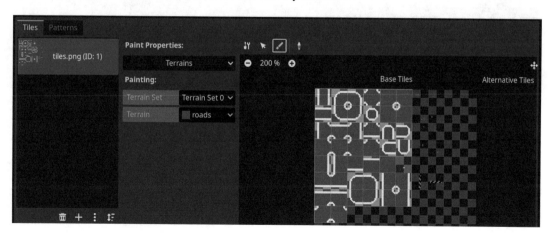

Bit masks

Notice how I have a blank tile in the terrain, which has no bits set. I arrived at this point through trial and error; so it's likely you'll need to experiment with the set_cells_ terrain_connect method for your game.

For instance, the final parameter is the ignore_blank_tiles method, which defaults to true. I had to set this to false to get the road tiles to connect. That, in combination with a completely blank (in appearance and bit mask) tile, results in a neat result.

Drawing the Players

Next up, we need to place the players on the map. We haven't actually made the players yet; so let's do that. I'm using the following artwork, but we'll only need parts of it:

Car sprites

It's tricky to see here, but the second line actually has the cars outlined. This is useful for car selection, as I have implemented in Bouncy Cars:

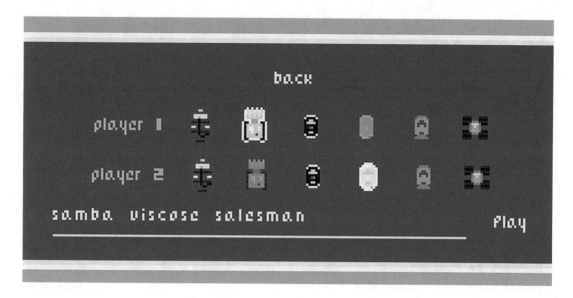

Selected cars

You can make as many of these vehicles as you like; but I'm going to stick to three for now. The base Player node needs a few child nodes that all of them will inherit. Here's what one of them looks like once it has a CollisionPolygon2D and Sprite2D:

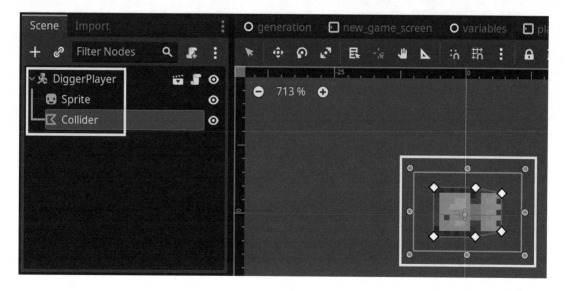

The digger

We can then place a random vehicle for both players at a random start location. Let's find a good starting position:

This is from nodes/screens/play_screen.gd

```
func get_start_cells() -> Dictionary:
    var start_cells = []

    for cell in map.cells:
        if cell.type == Types.cells.player_1_start:
            start_cells.push_back(cell)

    var player_1: Dictionary = start_cells[map.generator.randi() % start_
    cells.size()]
    var player_2: Dictionary

    for cell in map.cells:
        if cell.type == Types.cells.player_2_start:
            if cells_are_close(player_1, cell):
                player_2 = cell
                break

    return {
        "player_1": player_1,
        "player_2": player_2,
    }

func cells_are_close(player_1: Dictionary, player_2: Dictionary) -> bool:
    if player_1.x == player_2.x and (player_1.y == player_2.y - 1 or
    player_1.y == player_2.y + 1):
        return true

    if player_1.y == player_2.y and (player_1.x == player_2.x - 1 or
    player_1.x == player_2.x + 1):
        return true

    return false
```

These methods pick a random start cell for the first player and then find the closest start cell for the second player. The start positions need to be in the same row or column, or this code won't find the second start cell.

We can use these in the draw_players method to draw both players and rotate them to face the correct way with a rotate_players method:

This is from nodes/screens/play_screen.gd

```
@export var digger_scene : PackedScene
@export var fire_truck_scene : PackedScene
@export var monster_truck_scene : PackedScene

var player_1_vehicle : GamePlayer
var player_2_vehicle : GamePlayer

func draw_players() -> Dictionary:
    var start_cells := get_start_cells()

    var vehicle_scenes := [digger_scene, fire_truck_scene, monster_
    truck_scene]

    var player_1_tile_position : Vector2 = _tiles.map_to_
    local(Vector2(start_cells.player_1.x, start_cells.player_1.y))
    var player_1_start_position : Vector2 = player_1_tile_position + _
    tiles.position

    var player_1_vehicle_index : int = map.generator.randi() % vehicle_
    scenes.size()

    player_1_vehicle = vehicle_scenes[player_1_vehicle_index].instantiate()
    add_child(player_1_vehicle)

    player_1_vehicle.position = player_1_start_position

    vehicle_scenes.remove_at(player_1_vehicle_index)

    var player_2_tile_position : Vector2 = _tiles.map_to_
    local(Vector2(start_cells.player_2.x, start_cells.player_2.y))
    var player_2_start_position : Vector2 = player_2_tile_position + _
    tiles.position

    player_2_vehicle = vehicle_scenes[map.generator.randi() % vehicle_
    scenes.size()].instantiate()
    add_child(player_2_vehicle)
```

```
    player_2_vehicle.position = player_2_start_position

    var degrees := rotate_players(start_cells.player_1)

    return {
        "start_cells": start_cells,
        "degrees": degrees,
    }
func rotate_players(player_1 : Dictionary) -> int:
    var degrees := 0

    if (player_1.x < 5 and map.clockwise) or (player_1.x > 15 and not map.
    clockwise):
        degrees = -90

    if (player_1.x < 5 and not map.clockwise) or (player_1.x > 15 and map.
    clockwise):
        degrees = 90

    if (player_1.y < 5 and map.clockwise) or (player_1.y > 15 and not map.
    clockwise):
        degrees = 0

    if (player_1.y < 5 and not map.clockwise) or (player_1.y > 15 and map.
    clockwise):
        degrees = 180

    player_1_vehicle.rotation = deg_to_rad(degrees)
    player_2_vehicle.rotation = deg_to_rad(degrees)

    return degrees
```

There's a bunch happening, so let's break it down:

1. We start by picking a random vehicle for the first player using the generator instance returned by get_map.

2. We remove this vehicle from the pool for the second player so that the players have unique vehicles.

3. We calculate their position according to the start_position data.

4. We add both players to PlayScreen and have their position set.

5. We rotate the players based on the starting position of the first player. We assume that if they are close to the left- or right-hand side of the tile map, they need to face up or down.

6. If they're close to the top or the bottom of the tile map, then we face them left or right.

7. The start positions and initial rotation of the vehicles are important for working out the correct direction for travel later on.

This means you have to position your starting positions within the first five pixels of the left or top edges of your pre-drawn segments. We could determine these margins algorithmically, but I don't think it's worth the hassle.

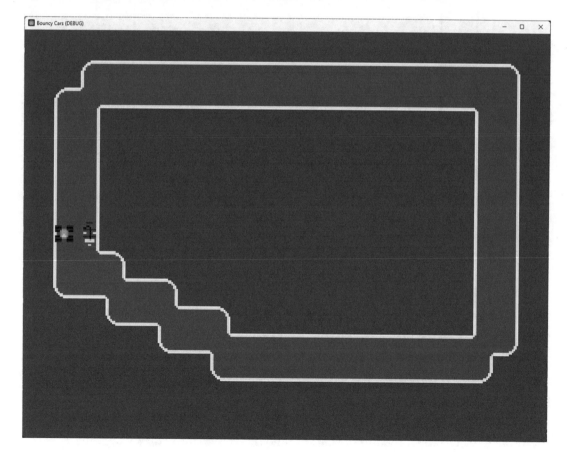

Drawing tiles and cars

Calculating Waypoints

Now we get to the part where we talk about waypoints: what they are and why we need them. Our segments have these light blue dots that we record as being waypoints.

In racing games like ours, where you can be facing either direction, it's common for the game to tell the player when they're going in the wrong direction.

In a game with generated maps, it can be tricky determining what the right way to go is. Let me describe how I hacked my way through it the first time so you can see my thought process.

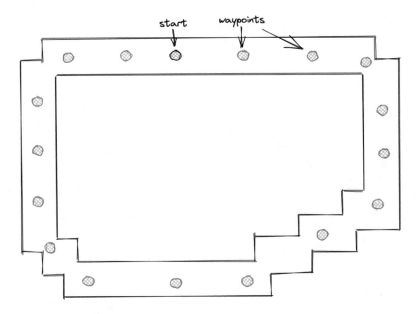

Invisible waypoints in the map

I started out drawing these invisible waypoints in the map, lining up with the waypoint pixels in the pre-drawn corners. Taking the direction into account, I'd then shoot a bullet from the first waypoint in the direction the players were facing.

If the direction was clockwise, I'd rotate a few degrees to the left; and if the direction was anticlockwise, I'd rotate a few to the right. This gave me a starting direction to fire an invisible bullet toward.

In increments of five degrees, if I hadn't hit anything with the invisible bullet, I'd rotate back toward the direction the cars should be facing, until I hit a waypoint.

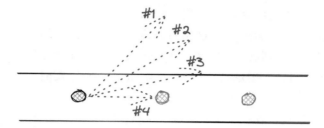

Firing bullets

Once I hit a waypoint, I'd add it to the list and start firing bullets from it, using the last angle as the new starting angle to fire the bullet.

These invisible bullets were fast, but they can't be too fast or they'll overshoot the waypoints. Because of this delay, I added a countdown timer to the start of the race, which was necessary to hide the bullet scan delay. This ended up being a nice feature of the game.

The Right Way to Do This

Little did I know, at the time, that I already had a better solution. I had to determine the correct "first" waypoint. I did by working out which waypoint had the smallest distance to the first player's starting position.

I just had to reuse the same logic to figure out what the next waypoint should be after that. Here's what that code should look like:

This is from nodes/screens/play_screen.gd

```
func reset() -> void:
    map = Generation.get_map(Variables.current_phrase)

    draw_map()
    var player_positions := draw_players()
    calculate_waypoints(player_positions)

var ordered_waypoint_positions : Array[Vector2] = []

func calculate_waypoints(player_positions: Dictionary) -> void:
    var unordered_waypoints = map.waypoints.duplicate() as Array
    var start_position : Vector2
```

123

```
while unordered_waypoints.size() > 0:
    if ordered_waypoint_positions.size() == 0:
        start_position = Vector2(player_positions.start_cells.
        player_1.x, player_positions.start_cells.player_1.y)
    else:
        start_position = ordered_waypoint_positions[ordered_waypoint_
        positions.size() - 1]

    var nearest_waypoint = unordered_waypoints[0]
    var nearest_waypoint_position = Vector2(nearest_waypoint.x,
    nearest_waypoint.y)

    for waypoint in unordered_waypoints:
        if ordered_waypoint_positions.size() < 2:
            if player_positions.degrees == 0 and waypoint.x < player_
            positions.start_cells.player_1.x:
                continue
            if player_positions.degrees == 90 and waypoint.y < player_
            positions.start_cells.player_1.y:
                continue
            if player_positions.degrees == 180 and waypoint.x > player_
            positions.start_cells.player_1.x:
                continue
            if player_positions.degrees == -90 and waypoint.y > player_
            positions.start_cells.player_1.y:
                continue

        var waypoint_position = Vector2(waypoint.x, waypoint.y)

        if waypoint_position.distance_squared_to(start_position) <
        nearest_waypoint_position.distance_squared_to(start_position):
            nearest_waypoint = waypoint
            nearest_waypoint_position = waypoint_position

    ordered_waypoint_positions.append(nearest_waypoint_position)
    unordered_waypoints.erase(nearest_waypoint)
```

Another huge method! Let's break it down:

1. We change the `reset` method to pass the starting positions and rotation to `calculate_waypoints`.

2. This, in turn, creates a copy of the unordered waypoints so that we can change this array in place.

3. While there are still unordered waypoints left, we loop through them and find the next nearest waypoint to the most recent ordered waypoint position.

4. If it's the first time we're doing this check, there won't be a last ordered waypoint; so we set this to the player's position.

5. If we're calculating the first couple waypoint positions, we want to eliminate all waypoints that are behind the players from the check so that we establish the clear direction to the next waypoint.

6. Once we calculate the nearest next waypoint, we add its position to the ordered waypoint position list and remove it from further checks.

This results in a list of ordered waypoint positions, where the first is the waypoint nearest in the direction the players should move and the last is the waypoint closest to their back.

Moving the Players

Let's add the ability for the first player to move around the track. There are a whole bunch of different ways to model their movement, but I found an interesting take. It's based on the physics surrounding a vehicle's wheel base, steering angle, and drag:

This is from nodes/players/player.gd

```
extends CharacterBody2D
class_name GamePlayer

@export var wheel_base := 30.0
@export var steering_angle := 90.0
```

```
@export var engine_power := 400.0
@export var friction := -0.9
@export var drag := -0.0015
@export var braking := -450.0
@export var max_speed_reverse := 150.0

var steer_angle: float
var acceleration := Vector2.ZERO

func _physics_process(delta: float) -> void:
    acceleration = Vector2.ZERO

    get_input()
    apply_friction()
    calculate_steering(delta)

    velocity += acceleration * delta
    var collided := move_and_slide()

func get_input():
    var turn = 0

    if Input.is_action_pressed("ui_left"):
        turn -= 1
    if Input.is_action_pressed("ui_right"):
        turn += 1

    steer_angle = turn * deg_to_rad(steering_angle)

    if Input.is_action_pressed("ui_up"):
        acceleration = transform.x * engine_power

    if Input.is_action_pressed("ui_down"):
        acceleration = transform.x * braking

func apply_friction():
    if velocity.length() < 5:
        velocity = Vector2.ZERO
```

```
    var friction_force = velocity * friction
    var drag_force = velocity * velocity.length() * drag

    if velocity.length() < 100:
        friction_force *= 3

    acceleration += drag_force + friction_force
func calculate_steering(delta):
    var rear_wheel = position - transform.x * wheel_base / 2.0
    var front_wheel = position + transform.x * wheel_base / 2.0

    rear_wheel += velocity * delta
    front_wheel += velocity.rotated(steer_angle) * delta

    var new_heading = (front_wheel - rear_wheel).normalized()

    var d = new_heading.dot(velocity.normalized())

    if d > 0:
        velocity = new_heading * velocity.length()

    if d < 0:
        velocity = -new_heading * min(velocity.length(), max_speed_reverse)

    rotation = new_heading.angle()
```

The movement happens in three stages:

1. Calculating the input that should affect the movement and
    increasing acceleration in response

2. Applying friction to slow the vehicle down over time

3. Applying a steering direction to the velocity

With this code in place, both vehicles move at the same time. That's definitely not the best behavior, though it is entertaining for a short while. We should add a set of controls that affect movement upon player creation so that we can only respond to them on the player that they apply to:

This is from nodes/players/player.gd

```
var controls := {
    "left": "ui_left",
    "right": "ui_right",
    "accelerate": "ui_up",
    "slow": "ui_down",
}

func get_input():
    var turn = 0

    if Input.is_action_pressed(controls.left):
        turn -= 1
    if Input.is_action_pressed(controls.right):
        turn += 1

    steer_angle = turn * deg_to_rad(steering_angle)

    if Input.is_action_pressed(controls.accelerate):
        acceleration = transform.x * engine_power

    if Input.is_action_pressed(controls.slow):
        acceleration = transform.x * braking
```

Then, we can disable the second player's controls by providing a different set of controls when we create it:

This is from nodes/screens/play_screen.gd

```
player_2_vehicle = vehicle_scenes[map.generator.randi() % vehicle_scenes.
size()].instantiate()

player_2_vehicle.controls = {
    "left": "ui_cancel",
    "right": "ui_cancel",
    "accelerate": "ui_cancel",
    "slow": "ui_cancel"
}

add_child(player_2_vehicle)
```

Warning the Players About Directions

Finally, we should use the waypoints we've calculated. Let's show something to the player to let them know what direction they should be travelling in. The ideal thing to use for this is an arrow that points to the next waypoint, so they can re-orient themselves:

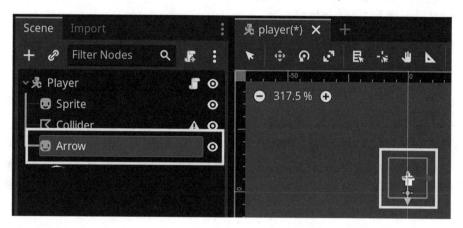

The waypoint arrow

We can reference this in the _physics_process method. We need to show the arrow (if required) and turn it toward the desired waypoint. This takes a bit of math and linear interpolation to look nice:

This is from nodes/players/player.gd

```
var show_waypoint := false
var waypoint_position : Vector2

@onready var _arrow := $Arrow as Sprite2D

func _physics_process(delta: float) -> void:
    if show_waypoint:
        _arrow.rotation = lerp(_arrow.rotation, get_angle_to(waypoint_
        position) + PI / 2, 1)
        _arrow.global_position = global_position.move_toward(waypoint_
        position, 20)
        _arrow.visible = true
    else:
```

```
        _arrow.visible = false

    acceleration = Vector2.ZERO

    get_input()
    apply_friction()
    calculate_steering(delta)

    velocity += acceleration * delta
    var collided := move_and_slide()
```

All that we should need to show the arrow pointing to the right place is tell the player to show the arrow and give it a position to point toward.

Unfortunately, this will take a bunch of code to achieve. We need to track the next waypoint the player is moving toward. If they are too far away from it, then we should show the arrow. If they get too close to it, then we need to pick the next waypoint in the sequence to set as their next:

This is from nodes/screens/play_screen.gd

```
var player_1_next_waypoint_index : int

func reset() -> void:
    map = Generation.get_map(Variables.current_phrase)

    draw_map()
    var player_positions := draw_players()
    calculate_waypoints(player_positions)

    player_1_next_waypoint_index = 0

func _physics_process(delta: float) -> void:
    var player_1_next_waypoint = ordered_waypoint_positions[player_1_next_
    waypoint_index]
    var player_1_next_waypoint_position := _tiles.map_to_
    local(Vector2(player_1_next_waypoint.x, player_1_next_waypoint.y))

    if player_1_vehicle.global_position.distance_to(player_1_next_waypoint_
    position) < 100:
        player_1_vehicle.show_waypoint = false
```

```
if player_1_vehicle.global_position.distance_to(player_1_next_
waypoint_position) < 50:
    player_1_next_waypoint_index += 1

    if player_1_next_waypoint_index >= ordered_waypoint_
    positions.size():
        player_1_next_waypoint_index = 0

    return
else:
    player_1_vehicle.show_waypoint = true
    player_1_vehicle.waypoint_position = player_1_next_waypoint_
    position
```

It would be a bit more efficient to do this with a timer, but the results would be the same.

Summary

This has been another huge chapter, putting our knowledge into practice. I've skimmed the surface of what it would take to produce a polished version of Bouncy Cars; but I've also shown you all the different parts of making a good procedural race track generator that you can base your own games on.

There are so many places you could take this project from here:

- You could wire up the second player's controls.

- You could add collisions to the road tiles so that the players need to stay inside the lines to win.

- You could add win/lose conditions and messaging.

- You could add more vehicles and decorations.

I could fill the rest of this book with these refinements, but I'll let you decide how much of that you would like to add to your game.

In the next chapter, we're going to move on to navigating within a generated world, not using the keyboard as we did here, but things like pathfinding and click to move.

CHAPTER 8

Navigating in Generated Levels

So far, all our player movement has been through the use of arrow keys or similar. We've yet to create a click-to-move system, or any sort of enemy or NPC (nonplayable character) movement. Before we can do that, we need to build a foundation for pathfinding.

That's going to be the focus of this chapter. We're going to look at how Godot handles pathfinding and how we can build maps with obstacles that the player must navigate around.

Getting Set Up

Let's create a new experiment in our experiment project, called `NavigationExperiment`. Follow all the same steps you did before to have this new experiment displayed as the default experiment. If you need a refresher, refer to Chapter 2 for how to set up new experiments.

Then, reuse any of the tile sets we've already used to create a basic `TileMap` and `TileSet` combo:

© Christopher Pitt 2023
C. Pitt, *Procedural Generation in Godot*, https://doi.org/10.1007/978-1-4842-8795-8_8

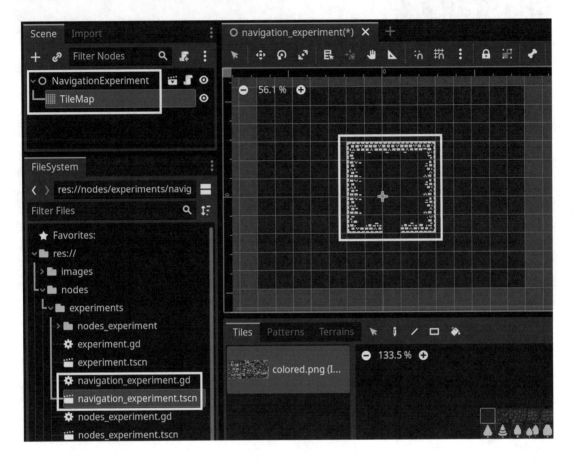

Creating the TileMap

Increase the *Transform* ➤ *Scale* of NavigationExperiment to 3 × 3 and change *Project Settings* ➤ *Window* values so that the graphics resize along with the window. 640 × 480 pixels seems like a good window size. Refer to the previous chapter if you get stuck.

This gives us a good starting point for the navigation work we're about to do.

Adding Basic Movement

Godot has a neat set of tools to help us work out the path we can take between points of interest. The main ones, which we need to add to our experiment, are NavigationRegion2D and NavigationAgent2D. The agent needs to be a child of the player sprite, while the region can be anywhere in the scene tree.

Once added, we will also need to enable *Avoidance* on the agent so that it can path around any obstacles, and *Max Speed* to 20 pixels per second:

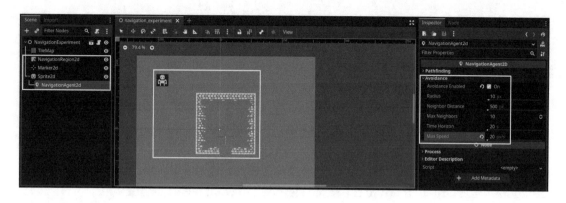

Regions and agents

I've set the player up as a Sprite2D, but you can use a node that has a position property. The code that controls or interacts with these nodes looks like this:

This is from experiments/navigation_experiment.gd

```
extends GameExperiment

@onready var _player := $Sprite2d as Sprite2D
@onready var _agent := $Sprite2d/NavigationAgent2d as NavigationAgent2D
@onready var _destination := $Marker2d as Marker2D

func _ready() -> void:
    _agent.velocity_computed.connect(
        func(velocity: Vector2) -> void:
            _player.global_position += velocity
    )

    _agent.set_target_location(_player.global_position)

    await get_tree().create_timer(1.0).timeout

    _agent.set_target_location(_destination.global_position)

func _physics_process(delta: float) -> void:
    var next_location := _agent.get_next_location()
    var next_velocity := next_location - _player.global_position
    _agent.set_velocity(next_velocity)
```

You can think of the `NavigationAgent2D` as the controller for the movement of the player. It communicates with the `NavigationServer` to work out the appropriate path between points of interest. It can also send movement or positional information back to the scene where things are moving.

In this case, we can listen for the `velocity_computed` signal and use the velocity it returns to move the player around the screen. To make sure this signal happens, check the *Avoidance Enabled* check box in the properties inspector pane.

Signals are the perfect place to use lambda functions, but we can also define named functions and connect them to the same signals. Do what feels best for you.

We need to call the agent's `get_next_location` method inside the physics process. This gets the next position on the path for the player to travel. It also allows the agent to check if there will be any collisions and adjust the path.

To work out what the new velocity should be, we take the next position along the path and subtract the player's position. This is the velocity the `NavigationAgent2D` needs to work out where to move next.

Adding Navigation to Tile Maps

It's not essential to have a `NavigationRegion2D` in order for this click-to-move functionality to work. It's just the simplest way to get started. If you prefer, you can also add this navigation region data to your tile maps.

Let's test this out by adding the data to our tile map:

1. Select the tile map and change *Navigation Visibility Mode* to *Force Show*.

2. Click the *Tile Set* drop-down, and scroll down to *Navigation Layers*.

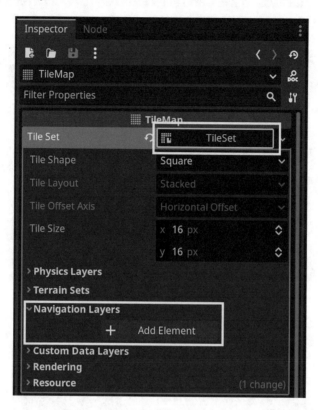

3. Click *Add Element*.

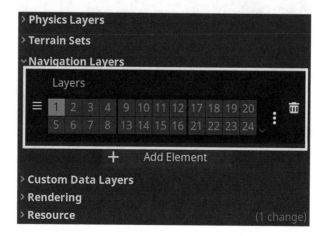

4. Click the *Tile Set* tab at the bottom of the screen.

5. Click the paint brush icon, and select the *Navigation Layer 0* we just created.

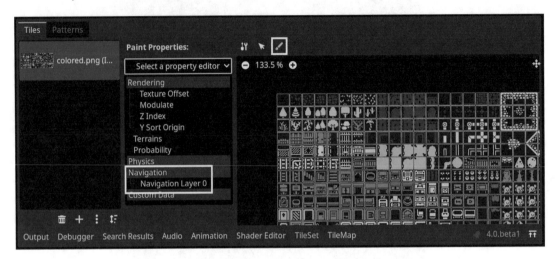

6. Click on the tiles that you want to be navigable.

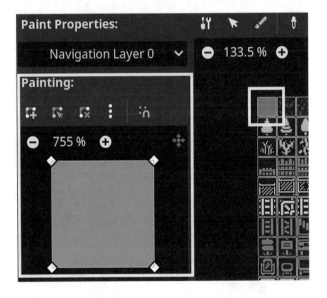

7. Once we remove the `NavigationRegion2D`, the map should resemble this:

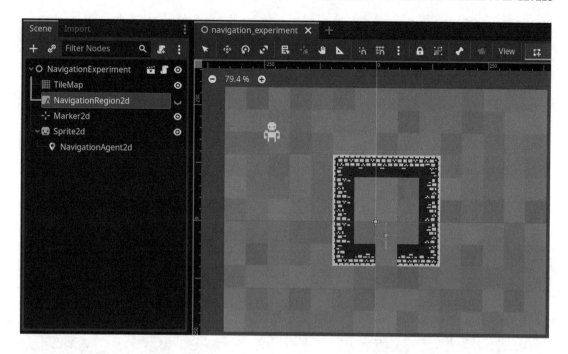

Navigation data in tile sets

We don't even have to change the code for the NavigationAgent2D to use this new navigation data. We only have to delete the NavigationRegion2D and re-run the game. The player character will now move around the walls instead of through them.

Adding Obstacle Nodes

We could build entire games using only these tile set navigation properties; but our games might need tile sets and obstacle nodes.

The simplest approach is to add more NavigationAgent2D nodes to the map. The player will then attempt to avoid them, though sometimes the pathing is a bit buggy:

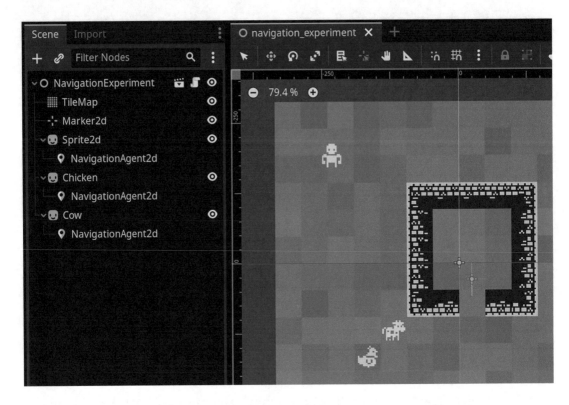

Avoidance with other NavigationAgent2D *nodes*

We can try to replicate this same navigation data using many NavigationRegion2D
nodes. It's going to be a pain in the butt to position them all next to each other and with
straight lines:

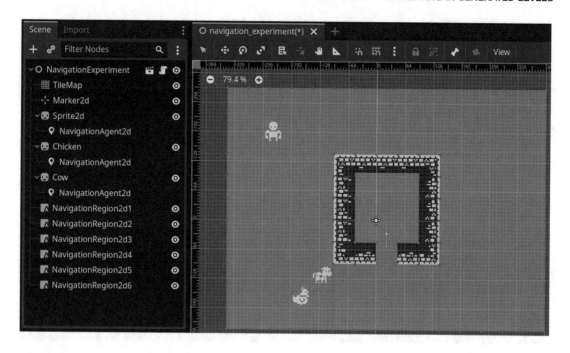

Navigation data in nodes

Furthermore, the navigation is still buggy. It would be better if we could use collision polygons to carve out non-navigable areas of the navigation rectangle.

Before we jump into the code required to do this, let's change our obstacles to `Area2D` nodes with `CollisionPolygon2D` colliders. We should also add another `Area2D` node for the walls:

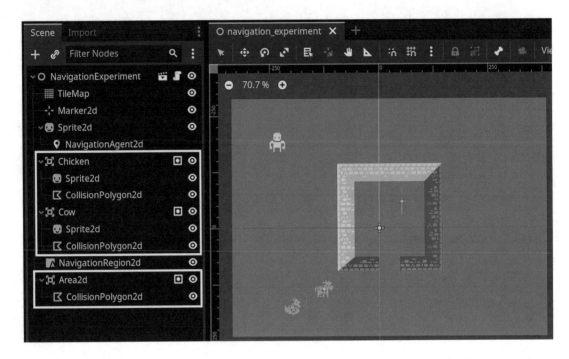

Adding colliders for non-navigable areas

Add each of these to a group. Make it something that you'll remember, which describes what the purpose of being in this group is:

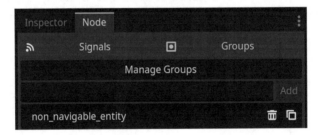

Adding non-navigable areas to the same group

Now, we can find these nodes and cut them out of the navigation region using code:

This is from experiments/navigation_experiment.gd

```
@onready var _region := $NavigationRegion2d as NavigationRegion2D

func cut_out_areas() -> void:
    var outlines := []
```

```
for node in get_tree().get_nodes_in_group("non_navigable_entity"):
    var node_outline := PackedVector2Array()

    var node_collider := node.get_node("CollisionPolygon2d") as
    CollisionPolygon2D
    var node_polygon := node_collider.get_polygon()

    for vertex in node_polygon:
        node_outline.append(node.transform * vertex)

    outlines.append(node_outline)

for outline in outlines:
    _region.navpoly.add_outline(outline)

_region.navpoly.make_polygons_from_outlines()
func _ready() -> void:
    cut_out_areas()

# ...
```

When the experiment loads up, we now call cut_out_areas, which loops through each of the grouped nodes and adds their outlines to an array.

We combine these with the outlines in the _region.navpoly so that they are excluded from the starting region polygon.

If you use this approach in your games, don't forget to call make_polygons_from_outlines, or your navigation region won't update.

Here's what this looks like, with *Debug* ➤ *Visible Navigation* enabled:

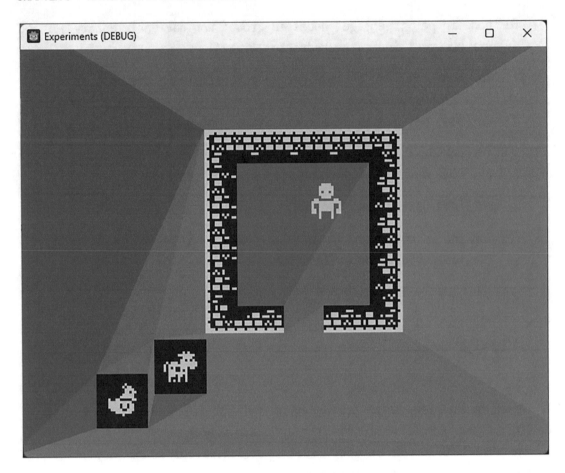

Cutting outlines out of a NavigationPolygon2D

Unfortunately, while the NavigationAgent2D movement is nicer, there are significant drawbacks to this approach, the main one being that the outlines can never touch.

Godot has this nasty habit of ignoring overlapping outlines. You're likely to see the error *NavigationPolygon: Convex partition failed!* If you leave gaps to avoid this, the player will move straight through the gaps, ignoring the intended route.

Merging Polygons

The most bullet-proof solution I've come across is to

1. Group overlapping polygons together

2. Combine them into single polygons

3. Add those polygons as outlines to the navpoly

It's a mission.

Let' start by creating a method to find intersecting polygons:

This is from experiments/navigation_experiment.gd

```
var auto_number = 0

func find_intersections(node, nodes, groups, group_id = null) ->
Dictionary:
    var node_collider := node.get_node("CollisionPolygon2d") as
    CollisionPolygon2D
    var node_polygon := node_collider.get_polygon()

    for other_node in nodes:
        if other_node == node:
            continue

        var other_node_collider := other_node.get_
        node("CollisionPolygon2d") as CollisionPolygon2D
        var other_node_polygon := other_node_collider.get_polygon()

        var result := Geometry2D.intersect_polygons(node_polygon * node.
        transform, other_node_polygon * other_node.transform)

        if result.size() > 0:
            if group_id == null:
                group_id = auto_number
                groups[group_id] = []
                groups[group_id].append(node)
                nodes.erase(node)
                auto_number += 1

            groups[group_id].append(other_node)
            nodes.erase(other_node)

    return {
        "nodes": nodes,
        "groups": groups,
    }
```

This method accepts a reference node, which is any node that has a CollisionPolygon2D in it. It also accepts an array of nodes to compare with. It loops through all the comparable nodes to see if any of them intersect with the subject node.

If it finds intersections, it adds both nodes to the groups array. If there is no group_id, it creates a new group from the subject node and all others from the list of comparable nodes that intersect with it.

Here's how you can think of it working:

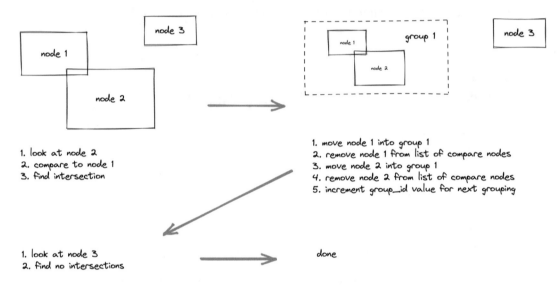

Grouping intersecting polygons

Let's also add a helper to simplify how we get outlines from collision polygons:

This is from experiments/navigation_experiment.gd

```
func get_outline(node) -> PackedVector2Array:
    var node_outline := PackedVector2Array()

    var node_collider := node.get_node("CollisionPolygon2d") as
    CollisionPolygon2D
    var node_polygon := node_collider.get_polygon()

    for vertex in node_polygon:
        node_outline.append(node.transform * vertex)

    return node_outline
```

We've already seen this code in action, but we're going to perform the same operation many times; so it's better to extract it to this helper method.

We can refactor the cut_out_areas method to combine intersecting groups of polygons into single polygons and add all the resulting outlines to the navpoly:

This is from experiments/navigation_experiment.gd

```
func cut_out_areas() -> void:
    var nodes := get_tree().get_nodes_in_group("non_navigable_entity")
    var groups := {}

    for node in nodes:
        var result := find_intersections(node, nodes, groups)
        nodes = result.nodes
        groups = result.groups

    for key in groups.keys():
        for node in groups[key]:
            var result := find_intersections(node, nodes, groups, key)
            nodes = result.nodes
            groups = result.groups

    for key in groups.keys():
        var outlines := []

        for node in groups[key]:
            outlines.append(get_outline(node))

        var combined = outlines[0]

        for outline in outlines.slice(1):
            combined = Geometry2D.merge_polygons(combined, outline)[0]

        _region.navpoly.add_outline(combined)
        _region.navpoly.make_polygons_from_outlines()

    for node in nodes:
        _region.navpoly.add_outline(get_outline(node))
        _region.navpoly.make_polygons_from_outlines()
```

1. We check the comparable node list to create the initial groups of intersecting nodes.

2. We follow this up by checking each intersecting group to make sure we've added all the nodes that overlap in the group. If we skipped this step, we could miss intersecting nodes due to the ordering of the initial comparable nodes array.

3. Once we have the final intersecting groups, we combine all their polygons into a single polygon per group.

4. These we add to the navpoly, along with a quick pass through all the non-intersecting polygons.

All this code combines to create a solution to the problem of overlapping outlines in a navpoly mesh. The resulting mesh means our player character will navigate around the obstacles:

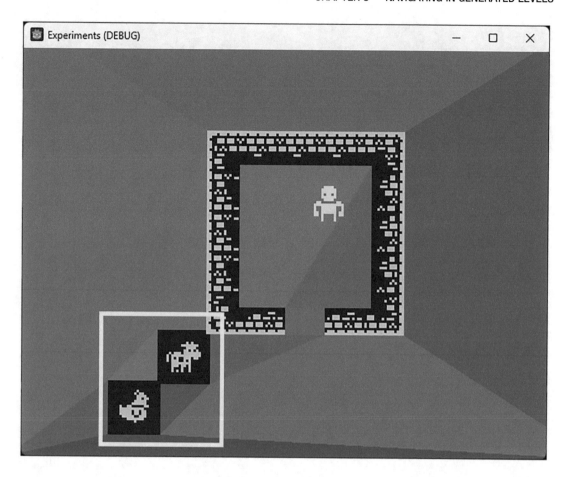

Combining polygons before adding them to the navpoly

This allows us to create obstacles dynamically and avoids the need to manually position `NavigationRegion2D` nodes. A handy trick, to be sure.

Summary

Navigation is one of those things that is easy to learn and difficult to master. Once you step outside of the simplest use case, things can and often do go awry.

Fortunately, we've come up with a solid solution to the problem of populating maps with obstacles. This will be super useful for the next game we make.

CHAPTER 9

Collective Nodes in Generated Maps

I don't know if you've noticed, but all our pixel-art-to-level code converts individual pixel into individual tiles or nodes. We've yet to take clusters of the same color pixels and convert them into a single complex node.

That's what we're going to tackle in this chapter. It's a trick that is going to come in handy for the next game we make. I want to take a quick detour to talk about the different approaches and skills we'll need to be able to do this.

Refreshing Our Memory

Do you remember the code that we used to draw nodes from pixel art?

This is from Chapter 5.

```
for row in layout:
    for cell in row:
        if tiles.has(cell):
            _tiles.set_cell(0, Vector2i(x, y), 0, tiles[cell])

        if nodes.has(cell):
            var new_node = nodes[cell].instantiate()
            _nodes.add_child(new_node)
            new_node.position = Vector2(x * 16, y * 16)
```

This code shows the 1:1 relationship between pixels in the layout image and the nodes or tiles they represent in a map. I want us to develop this idea further.

C. Pitt, *Procedural Generation in Godot*, https://doi.org/10.1007/978-1-4842-8795-8_9

Let's create a new experiment. We'll call this one `CollectiveNodesExperiment`. Be sure to set it as the experiment that loads on `PlayScreen`.

To this, we'll add a couple `OptionButton` nodes for width and height. We could use `LineEdit` nodes, but that would allow invalid inputs. I think it's better to stick with the safer list of allowed values:

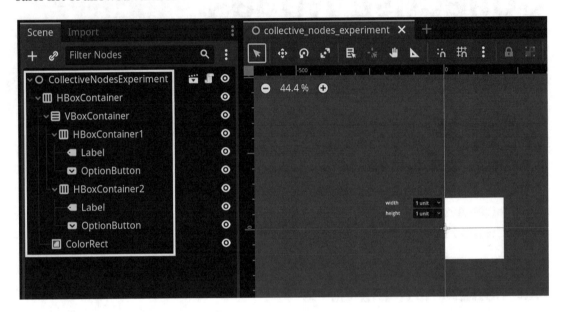

Creating UI for our experiment

I've gone ahead and set minimum widths on the `HBoxContainer`, `VBoxContainer`, and `ColorRect` nodes. Being descendants of a `Node2D`, they cannot assume their size so they begin at 0px width and 0px height.

I've added the following units to the `OptionButton` nodes, but you can add different ones if you prefer:

- 1 unit

- 2 units

- 3 units

You can think of these values as they relate to the pixels of whatever pixel art image we are drawing from. We're not actually going to attach these to an image, but you should be well familiar with how that works by now.

As either of these `OptionButton` nodes changes, we can call a render method, which can switch out the visible nodes:

This is from experiments/collective_nodes_experiment.gd

```
extends GameExperiment

var width := 1
var height := 1

func _ready() -> void:
    render()

func _on_width_option_button_item_selected(index: int) -> void:
    width = index + 1
    render()

func _on_height_option_button_item_selected(index: int) -> void:
    height = index + 1
    render()

func render() -> void:
    print(str(width) + " wide, " + str(height) + " high")
```

Don't forget to link these methods up to their respective nodes:

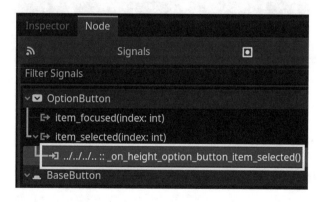

Connecting OptionButton signals

Now, when either of the `OptionButton` nodes changes, we should see a debug message describing the intended width and height.

Selecting the Appropriate Node(s)

The basic idea behind a node like this is that we want to show or hide sprites and colliders based on how high and wide the node should be. We're actually going to have many possible variations but only display one that fits the intended size.

Let's create a few variations:

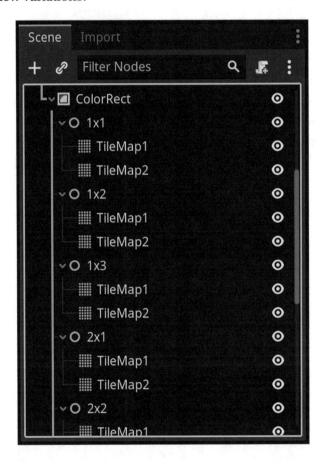

Tile map variations

The configuration I've chosen is a bunch of Node2D nodes, nested below the ColorRect node. Each contains possible variations matching the name of their parent.

So the TileMap nodes below 1x3 would all be one unit wide and three units high. They might have a different visual style and colliders; but they fit within the size dictated by their parent Node2D.

We can select from among these by composing the name of the intended Node2D:

This is from experiments/collective_nodes_experiment.gd

```
@onready var _color_rect := $HBoxContainer/ColorRect as ColorRect

func render() -> void:
    for group in _color_rect.get_children():
        for child in (group as Node2D).get_children():
            (child as TileMap).visible = false

    var intended_name := str(width) + "x" + str(height)
    var intended_node := _color_rect.get_node(intended_name)
    var index = randi() % intended_node.get_child_count()

    (intended_node.get_child(index) as TileMap).visible = true
```

We could achieve this in many different ways:

1. Giving every `TileMap` a group of the composite name, like `tile_1x1`, and finding all nodes within the same group to select from

2. Adding all `TileMap` nodes to an exported array of node paths

The bottom line is that we're achieving a level of randomization with the constraints of an intended width and height.

This will allow us to tell a "house" node how wide and high we want it to be. It'll have a fixed size based on a cluster of pixels in our pixel art layout image, but still be somewhat random.

We don't have to stick to using `TileMap` nodes, either. We've spent an equal amount of time learning about nodes and colliders so we could show or hide node trees. You can choose the approach you prefer, or mix and match.

Summary

I hope this short chapter has given you a little palette cleanse before we dive into recreating another game.

In the next chapter, we're going to use the navigation and collective nodes to make something even more intricate than Bouncy Cars.

If you're looking for more of a challenge, try to change the drawing code, from Chapter 4 or 5 or 7, to account for clusters of pixels. We'll see what this code looks like in the next chapter, so don't stress if you can't figure it out immediately.

CHAPTER 10

Recreating Invasion

Invasion is a game I recently built, inspired by world events. It's a strategy game, where you try to lead survivors through a war zone.

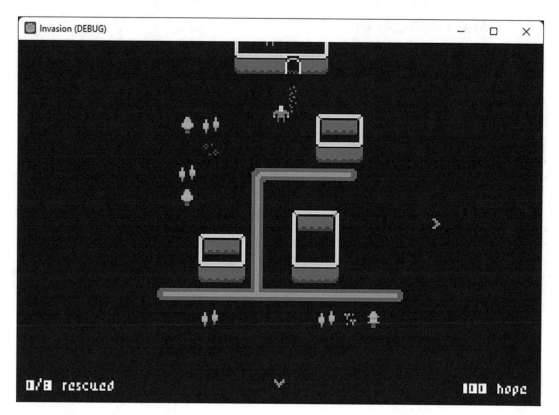

Invasion (2022)

It has a surprising amount of depth, despite being capable of running on a phone or tablet. That's thanks to the click-to-move navigation and solid content generation code.

In this chapter, we're going to rebuild this game, putting into practice everything we've learned so far.

© Christopher Pitt 2023
C. Pitt, *Procedural Generation in Godot*, https://doi.org/10.1007/978-1-4842-8795-8_10

Getting Set Up

We've been through this process quite a few times now, so I'm not going to go super deep into any of it. Let's summarize the steps we should follow and then let's talk about polish:

1. We need to set up a folder structure that supports our screens, globals, scenery, and actors.

2. Our screens should extend a base scene so that we can add screen switching, transitions, and mobile support.

3. We should base our level generation on pixel art, though we can forgo a seeding system.

4. The scenery code should account for collective nodes, which we can see in the preceding screenshot.

I'll go through each of these, with screenshots.

Screens

Head over to *Project* ➤ *Project Settings*, and adjust the *Viewport, Override,* and *Stretch* settings:

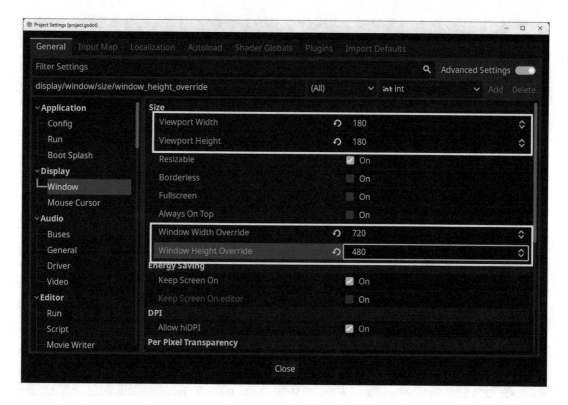

Adjusting screen size

With this done, I set up the usual `MarginContainer`-based screen system:

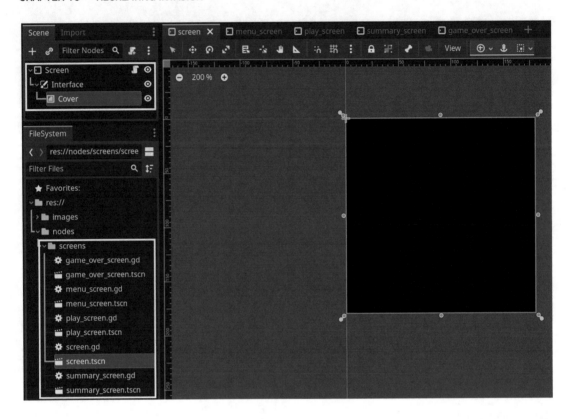

Screens for the game

I've added a new CanvasLayer → ColorRect node combination. We're going to use this for a fancy screen transition, but first, we need to add the screen switching and menu buttons.

As before, we need to define the list of screens and their scene files:

This is from nodes/globals/constants.gd

```
extends Node
class_name Types

@export var game_over_scene : PackedScene
@export var menu_scene : PackedScene
@export var play_scene : PackedScene
@export var summary_scene : PackedScene

enum screens {
    game_over,
```

```
    menu,
    play,
    summary,
}

@onready var screen_scenes := {
    screens.game_over: game_over_scene,
    screens.menu: menu_scene,
    screens.play: play_scene,
    screens.summary: summary_scene,
}
```

We can reference these in the standard screen switching code we've written a few times:

This is from nodes/globals/screens.gd

```
extends Node

var root = null
var current_screen := Types.screens.menu
var current_screen_node : GameScreen
var is_changing_screen := false

func _ready() -> void:
    root = get_tree().get_root()
    current_screen = Types.screens.menu
    current_screen_node = root.get_children().back()

func change_screen(new_screen: Types.screens) -> void:
    if is_changing_screen:
        return

    is_changing_screen = true

    var new_screen_node : GameScreen = Constants.screen_scenes[new_screen].
    instantiate()
    await load_new_screen(new_screen_node, new_screen)

    is_changing_screen = false
```

```
func load_new_screen(new_screen_node: GameScreen, new_screen: Types.
screens) -> void:
    current_screen_node.queue_free()
    root.add_child(new_screen_node)

    current_screen = new_screen
    current_screen_node = new_screen_node
```

We can connect to this code from our MenuScreen buttons. Speaking of which, I want to add a quit button to our main menu.

Only this time, I want to explore a new way of finding the button, so we can hide it when we export the game to platforms that don't support quitting.

The most common way we've referenced nodes is with the @onready var _button := $Path/To/Button notation. There's another that doesn't hard-code the relationships between the button and its parent nodes. If we right-click on the button node and select *Access as Scene Unique Name*, we can reference it using this new %Syntax.

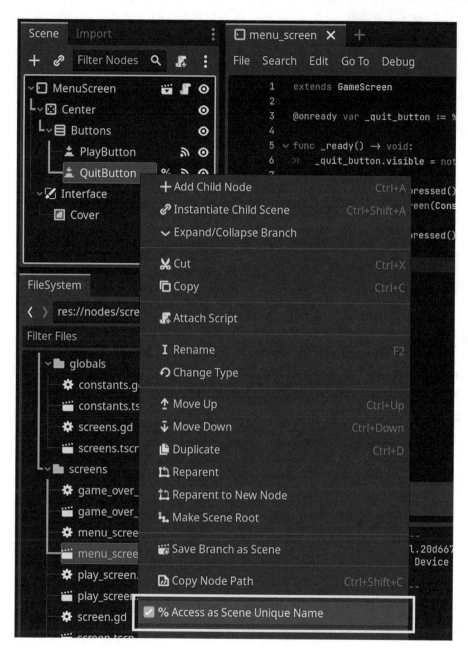

Using scene-unique names

Our menu code looks like this:

This is from nodes/screens/menu_screen.gd

```
extends GameScreen

@onready var _quit_button := %QuitButton as Button

func _ready() -> void:
    _quit_button.visible = not OS.has_feature("HTML5")

func _on_play_button_pressed() -> void:
    Screens.change_screen(Constants.screens.play)

func _on_quit_button_pressed() -> void:
    get_tree().quit()
```

Transitions

I had to make the Cover node invisible to see what I was doing with the menu nodes. Let's add the screen transition code so we can hide Cover with a fancy shader.

I like to implement transitions with signals and hooks. Hooks are methods with special names that our code can call automatically. The flow can be quite confusing at first:

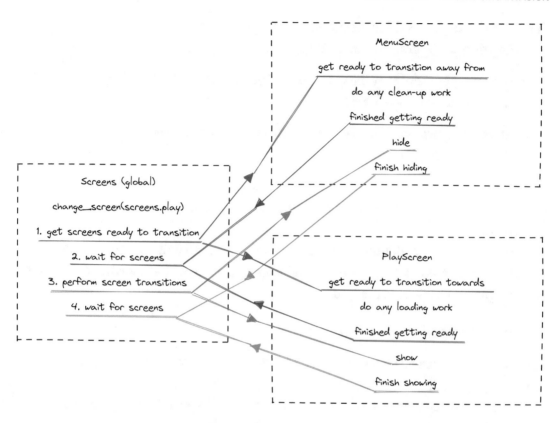

Signals and actions when switching screens

This requires adding signals to the screens we're going to switch between, which is where the common parent class comes in handy:

This is from nodes/screens/screen.gd

```
extends MarginContainer
class_name GameScreen

signal did_prepare_to_hide
signal did_hide_with_transition
signal did_prepare_to_show
signal did_show_with_transition

func prepare_to_hide(next_screen : Types.screens) -> void:
    did_prepare_to_hide.emit()
```

```
func hide_with_transition(next_screen : Types.screens) -> void:
    did_hide_with_transition.emit()

func prepare_to_show(previous_screen : Types.screens) -> void:
    did_prepare_to_show.emit()

func show_with_transition(previous_screen : Types.screens) -> void:
    did_show_with_transition.emit()
```

We need to call these from our screen switching code. We should prepare the screens for showing and hiding and only free the old screen when all the transitions have happened.

The methods we've defined on the Screen node immediately emit their related signals, so there aren't any animations. We're going to change that shortly. For now, let's call the appropriate Screen methods:

This is from nodes/globals/screens.gd

```
func load_new_screen(new_screen_node: GameScreen, new_screen: Types.
screens) -> void:
    current_screen_node.call_deferred("prepare_to_hide", new_screen)
    await current_screen_node.did_prepare_to_hide

    current_screen_node.call_deferred("hide_with_transition", new_screen)
    await current_screen_node.did_hide_with_transition

    current_screen_node.queue_free()
    root.add_child(new_screen_node)

    new_screen_node.call_deferred("prepare_to_show", current_screen)
    await new_screen_node.did_prepare_to_show

    new_screen_node.call_deferred("show_with_transition", current_screen)
    await new_screen_node.did_show_with_transition

    current_screen = new_screen
    current_screen_node = new_screen_node
```

We can await custom signals in the same way as we await signals from built-in classes and methods. We can shuffle these calls and awaits around if we wanted the operations to happen in parallel.

The animation we're going for only makes sense if they show and hide in sequence, though.

Adding Shaders

Let's make the ColorRect appear and disappear with a fancy shader. I'm by no means a shader expert; but I have put together a simple effect that will work for us.

Selecting the ColorRect node, we can go to *Material ➤ New ShaderMaterial ➤ New Shader*. Save the resulting file anywhere, and then switch to the Shader Editor tab (on the bottom of the window).

We can use the following shader code:

This is from nodes/screens/screen.gdshader

```
shader_type canvas_item;

uniform float amount : hint_range(0, 1) = 0.0;
uniform float bandSize = 40.0;

void fragment() {
    float yFraction = fract(FRAGCOORD.y / bandSize);
    float yDistance = abs(yFraction - 0.5);

    if (yDistance + UV.y > amount * 2.0) {
        discard;
    }
}
```

In short, this shader says that as the amount reaches 1.0, more of the screen should be covered in the black banding:

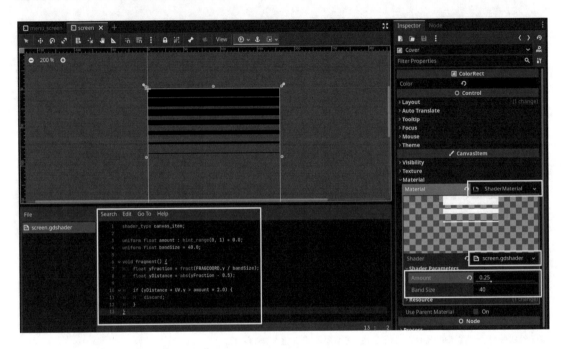

Adjusting shader amount in the property inspector

We can tween this amount property during the screen transitions. When we're hiding a screen, we should increase the amount to `1.0`, and when we're showing a screen, we should do the opposite.

This is from nodes/screens/screen.gd

```
@onready var _cover := %Cover as ColorRect

var duration := 1.0

func prepare_to_hide(next_screen : Types.screens) -> void:
    _cover.material.set_shader_parameter("amount", 0.1)
    did_prepare_to_hide.emit()

func hide_with_transition(next_screen : Types.screens) -> void:
    var tween = get_tree().create_tween()
    tween.tween_method(func(value): _cover.material.set_shader_
    parameter("amount", value), 0.0, 1.0, duration)
    await tween.finished

    did_hide_with_transition.emit()
```

```
func prepare_to_show(previous_screen : Types.screens) -> void:
    did_prepare_to_show.emit()

func show_with_transition(previous_screen : Types.screens) -> void:
    var tween = get_tree().create_tween()
    tween.tween_method(func(value): _cover.material.set_shader_
    parameter("amount", value), 1.0, 0.0, duration)
    await tween.finished

    did_show_with_transition.emit()
```

This is an interesting combination of lambda syntax and procedural tweening. We prepare to show Cover by setting its amount parameter to 0.0, and then we tween this value to 1.0 as we hide the screen.

Planning Room Generation

Each Invasion level has some connected rooms. We can use a lot of the same code we created for Bouncy Cars.

Layouts for rooms

We can use a layout image like this, where each room is 11 × 11 pixels:

- Purple pixels are paths.

- Red pixels are houses.

- Green pixels are trees.

- Gray pixels are gravestones.

The process for making a map from these layouts is as follows:

1. Convert pixel data into cell data.

2. Combine clusters of pixels into single cells.

3. Create node instances for each cell.

The added complication is that we want to generate adjoining "rooms" that the player can travel between. The player should spawn in one of the rooms. This starting room should also contain the "safe house" to lead survivors to.

A different room should contain the safe house, which acts as a way for the player to complete the level.

We can visualize the rooms like this:

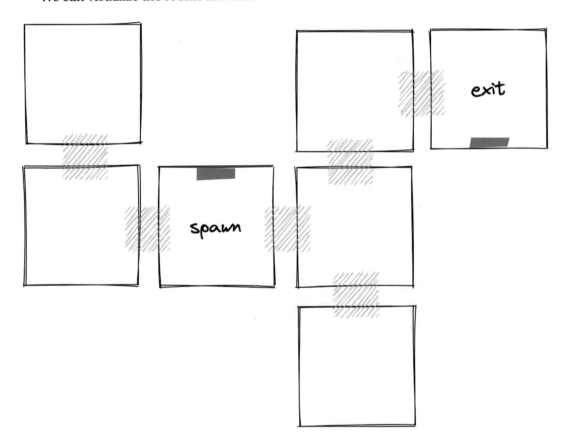

Connected rooms

Let's start by creating a single room so that we can get the code for pixels → nodes out of the way. Here are the nodes I have in my Room scene:

We need to do quite a bit of setup for the rooms to function. I'm going to show you a hectic screenshot and then break down each part in sections:

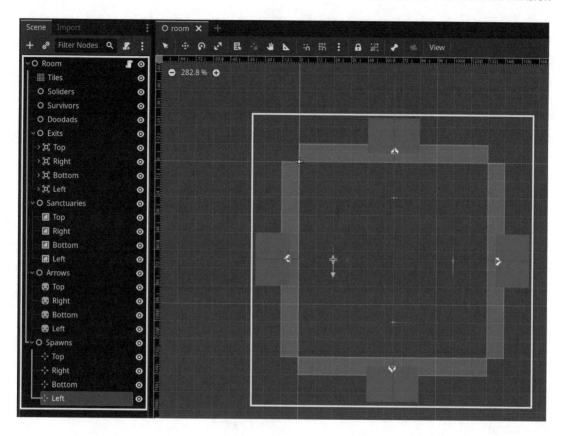

Room scene

You can save this scene to the nodes folder and attach an empty script to it. I have the grid showing and the snap positions set to 12 × 12 pixels. The guides are at 66 pixels on each axis. The exit area colliders are 11 grid cells wide, and their center is on 66 pixels.

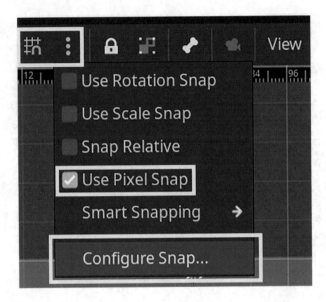

Snapping to the grid

Tile Map

I'm basing this tile set on a kenney.nl asset pack that I've extracted and modified various tiles from:

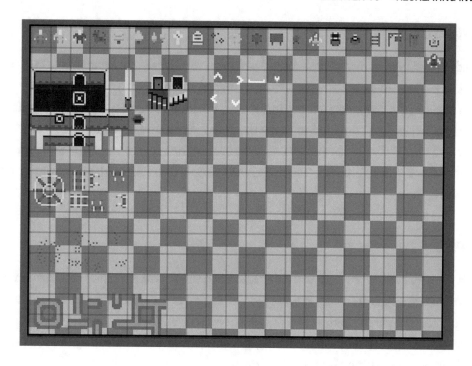

Room sprites

Each of these modified sprites is 12 × 12 pixels; so I've set up a tile set sprite for those dimensions and created the TileSet to have a road terrain. I had planned to use more of these tiles in the pixel layouts, but I found these too noisy in the final game.

Feel free to use them in yours, as long as you can set up new pixel colors and adjust the generation code to match.

12 × 12 pixel tiles, in an 11 × 11 unit layout, means each room has a size of 132 × 132 pixels. This is smaller than our 180 × 180 screen size, but we'll center the rooms and the *Aspect* settings will scale them up to fill the center of the screen.

Exits

As the player moves to the edges of the screen, we need to transition them into the adjacent room if this exists. I've set up four Area2D nodes, with CollisionShape2D children, to be able to detect this transition.

These can be on the edges of the level so that walking to the edge will start the transition. We still need to code that part, though.

Sanctuaries

When the level begins, the player should start in a room that has a sanctuary in it. This is where the player needs to bring survivors to rescue them.

We also need a visible sanctuary in the room through which the player exits. These can look different, but I decided to make them look the same in my build of the game.

They're blue `ColorRect` nodes in the screenshot, but you're welcome to make them custom nodes if you so choose. Keeping things simple to focus on the important parts of this chapter.

Arrows

If there are adjacent rooms, we want to indicate to the player that they can travel in the direction of the adjacent room. Rooms won't have an adjacent room on every side, so the idea is to hide the arrows if they aren't present on that edge of the room.

These overlapping nodes might look strange, but we'll hide them by default and show them when nothing else is in that position.

Spawns

We need to show where the player can spawn when the level starts and when they move from room to room. This can be hard-coded in a script, but I prefer a visual indicator.

That's why I've created a `Spawns  Node2D` to hold four `Marker2D` nodes. Our scripts can use the position of these visual indicators to work out where the player should enter a room, or where they should spawn.

It's best that these positions do not intersect any doodads in our pixel art layout image. Otherwise, the player might be stuck in the position they spawn in. Plan your layout images so there is open space for these markers.

The Remaining Nodes

All the remaining nodes are placeholders for where we'll add doodads, soldiers, and survivors. We could add them all to the same parent node; but that makes runtime debugging a bit harder.

Generating One Room

Now that we've taken care of the structure for each room, we need to write some code to handle drawing the tiles and doodads into each room. This code should take a random room layout and work out which pixels are nodes and which are tiles.

The layouts in the pixel art image are already horizontally flipped. I don't want to vertically flip them because it would complicate the buildings.

First, we need to set up some constants:

This is from nodes/globals/constants.gd

```
@export var tree_scene : PackedScene
@export var grave_scene : PackedScene
@export var house_scene : PackedScene
@export var grass_scene : PackedScene

enum drawables {
    tree,
    grave,
    house,
    grass,
    path,
}

@onready var drawable_scenes := {
    drawables.tree: tree_scene,
    drawables.grave: grave_scene,
    drawables.house: house_scene,
    drawables.grass: grass_scene,
}

var drawable_colors := {
    drawables.tree: "22c55e",
    drawables.grave: "71717a",
    drawables.house: "ef4444",
    drawables.grass: "fbbf24",
    drawables.path: "a855f7",
}
```

```
var drawable_tiles := [
    drawables.path,
]

var drawable_groups := [
    drawables.house,
]

var number_of_layouts := 8
var layout_width := 11
var sprite_width := 12
```

This is all quite like Chapter 7, but we're also adding nodes into the mix. We need to make a scene for each of those exports.

All the drawables extend on this node and code:

This is from nodes/drawables/drawable.gd

```
extends Node2D
class_name GameDrawable

var drawable_size : Vector2i

func set_drawable_size(size : Vector2i) -> void:
    drawable_size = size
```

Normally, we'd use the property syntax to define this kind of setter. It's simpler, instead, to use a method that we can override it in the child classes that need to.

The tree, grave, and grass scenes are all similar and simple. Let me show you what one of them looks like, and you can follow this pattern for the others.

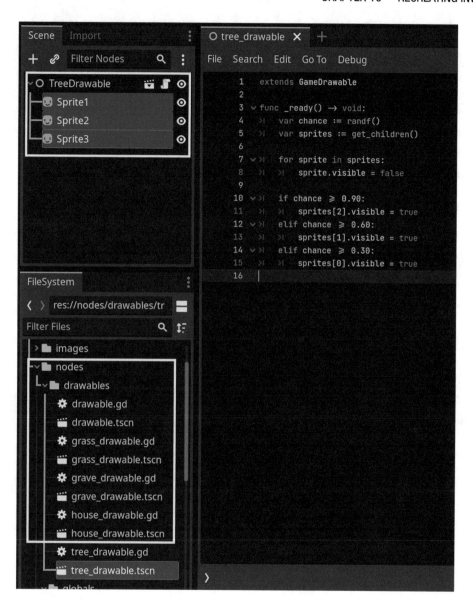

Showing a random tree sprite

We followed a similar approach in Chapter 2. This gives roughly a 1/10 chance for the one tree design to show, a 4/10 chance for the next, and a 7/10 chance for the third.

The graves and grass follow the same approach, with different sprites and percentages. I use low probability for those, so the room isn't too noisy.

Here's that code in a more readable format:

This is from nodes/drawables/tree_drawable.gd

```
extends GameDrawable

func _ready() -> void:
    var chance := randf()
    var sprites := get_children()

    for sprite in sprites:
        sprite.visible = false

    if chance >= 0.90:
        sprites[2].visible = true
    elif chance >= 0.60:
        sprites[1].visible = true
    elif chance >= 0.30:
        sprites[0].visible = true
```

The houses are a bit more complicated, but they follow the approach we learned about in the previous chapter:

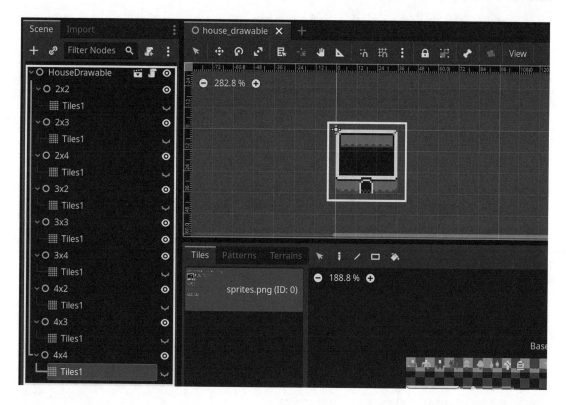

Showing variable-size houses

I went ahead and created a TileMap node in each of the sizes our layouts support. There are nine of them, most of which we need to hide via script. We should only be showing the one required by the size given during the generation phase. Here's how we do that:

This is from nodes/drawables/house_drawable.gd

```
extends GameDrawable

func set_drawable_size(size : Vector2i) -> void:
    super.set_drawable_size(size)

    for group in get_children():
        for variation in group.get_children():
            variation.visible = false
```

```
var intended_name := str(drawable_size.x) + "x" + str(drawable_size.y)
var intended_node := get_node(intended_name)
var index = randi() % intended_node.get_child_count()

(intended_node.get_child(index) as TileMap).visible = true
```

We can call the `set_drawable_size` method, on the parent class, with the super keyword. Next, we can plan an instance of the Room in the PlayScreen:

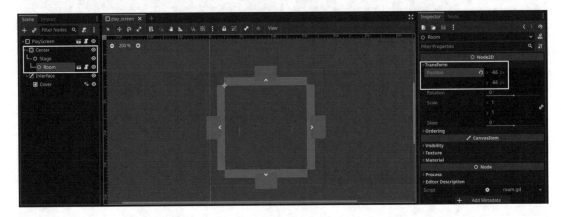

Adding a test Room instance to PlayScreen

Notice how I've put the Room at -66 × -66 pixels. This is half the width and height, so it is in the center of the screen.

If we launch the game, we should see the sanctuaries and arrows. Let's work on the code that draws doodads and tiles.

We'll need three methods:

- Generating a random room layout from the pixel art layout file

- Drawing `TileMap` road tiles

- Drawing drawables for everything else

The layout method looks much like the ones we've made before:

This is from nodes/globals/generation.gd

```
extends Node

@export var layout_texture : Texture2D
```

```
func _ready() -> void:
    randomize()

func get_room_layout() -> Array:
    var image := layout_texture.get_image()
    var offset : int = (randi() % Constants.number_of_layouts) * Constants.
    layout_width
    var room := []

    for y in range(Constants.layout_width):
        var row := []

        for x in range(Constants.layout_width):
            var drawable_type : Types.drawables
            var pixel_color = image.get_pixel(x + offset, y).to_html(false)

            for type in Constants.drawable_colors.keys():
                if pixel_color == Constants.drawable_colors[type]:
                    drawable_type = type

            row.push_back(drawable_type)

        room.push_back(row)

    return room
```

This gives us a 2D array of tile and node types. We can pass to the other methods we need to make. First up, the TileMap drawing method:

This is from nodes/globals/generation.gd

```
func add_room_tiles(tilemap : TileMap, layout : Array) -> void:
    var tiles : Array[Vector2i] = []

    for y in range(Constants.layout_width):
        for x in range(Constants.layout_width):
            if not layout[y][x] in Constants.drawable_tiles:
                continue

            tiles.push_back(Vector2i(x, y))

    tilemap.set_cells_terrain_connect(0, tiles, 0, 0, false)
```

This is like the one we made for Bouncy Cars. We can pair it with a method that creates and places drawable nodes:

This is from nodes/globals/generation.gd

```
func add_room_doodads(node : Node2D, layout : Array) -> void:
    var ignored : Array[Vector2i] = []

    for y in range(Constants.layout_width):
        for x in range(Constants.layout_width):
            var current : Types.drawables = layout[y][x]

            if ignored.has(Vector2i(x, y)):
                continue

            if not Constants.drawable_scenes.keys().has(current):
                continue

            var drawable_size : Vector2i

            if current in Constants.drawable_groups:
                var w := 0
                var h := 0

                for i in range(5):
                    if layout[y + i][x] != current:
                        break

                    for j in range(5):
                        if layout[y + i][x + j] != current:
                            break

                        ignored.append(Vector2i(x + j, y + i))

                        if i == 0:
                            w += 1

                    h += 1

                drawable_size = Vector2i(w, h)

            var drawable = Constants.drawable_scenes[current].instantiate()
            as GameDrawable
```

```
node.add_child(drawable)

drawable.set_drawable_size(drawable_size)

drawable.position = Vector2(
    x * Constants.sprite_width,
    y * Constants.sprite_width,
)
```

This is the code I hinted at, toward the end of the previous chapter:

- We loop through the rows and columns (y → x), ignoring all TileMap types and pixels we've already accounted for as part of a cluster.

- We do a bit more processing for each type in the drawable_ groups array.

  - We loop from 0 → 4 to see if there are matching cell types to the right.

  - We loop from 0 → 4 to see if there are matching cell types downward.

- We combine these into a new drawable_size variable and add individual cells to the ignore list.

- Once we've gone through all the cells, we create new nodes and assign the drawable_size to each.

With these methods in place, we can adjust the Room script so that it generates itself:

This is from nodes/room.gd

```
extends Node2D
class_name GameRoom

@onready var _tiles := %Tiles as TileMap
@onready var _doodads := %Doodads as Node2D

func _ready() -> void:
    var layout : Array = Generation.get_room_layout()

    Generation.add_room_tiles(_tiles, layout)
    Generation.add_room_doodads(_doodads, layout)
```

The room is now responsible for adding its own tiles and nodes. The results are quite lovely:

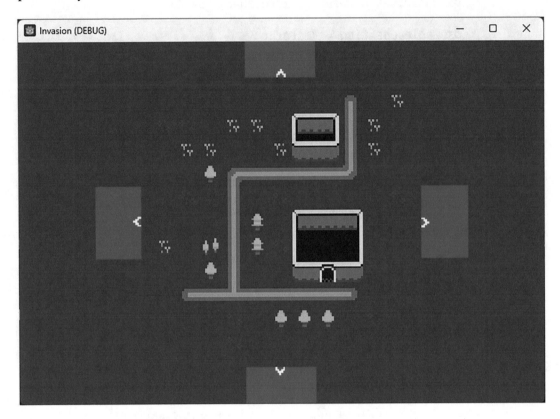

Rooms that draw themselves

Feel free to add as many other decorations as you like. One thing I like about our houses is that we can create any number of variations. These could include houses that have second floors and yards. The tile set has some lovely decorations to achieve this.

Generating Many Rooms

Now that we can create a single room, it's time to create a few and link them together. This should include the following details:

- The starting room must have a rescue sanctuary in it.

- There should be a limited number of rooms, branching out from it.

- The final room should have an exit sanctuary in it.

- The arrows should only be visible on edges where there is an adjacent room present.

Let's build this function in stages, starting with the code to generate the first room:

This is from nodes/globals/generation.gd

```
func make_rooms(parent) -> void:
    Variables.room_positions_available = []
    Variables.room_positions_taken = []
    Variables.rooms = []

    var first_room = Constants.room_scene.instantiate() as GameRoom
    parent.add_child(first_room)
    first_room.room_position = Vector2i(0, 0)
    first_room.room_type = Constants.rooms.first
    first_room.position = Vector2(-66, -66)

    var rooms_left = Constants.number_of_rooms - 1
```

This code begins by resetting variables in a new global: `Variables`. Here's what the script for that global looks like:

This is from nodes/globals/variables.gd

```
extends Node

var room_positions_available : Array[Vector2i]= []
var room_positions_taken : Array[Vector2i] = []
var rooms : Array[GameRoom] = []
```

These arrays are typed to only allow values of the defined types. The `make_rooms` method continues by creating a new instance of the room scene. The `Constants` script also gets a few new properties:

This is from nodes/globals/constants.gd

```
@export var room_scene : PackedScene

var number_of_rooms := 8
```

185

```
enum rooms {
    first,
    other,
    last,
}

enum room_neighbors {
    top,
    right,
    bottom,
    left,
}
```

Don't forget to reference the room scene through the property inspector or you'll get a nasty error message when running this code, something like *Nonexistent function 'instantiate' in base 'Nil'.*

Once we create and position the first room, we can get all the potential neighbors. This requires a few methods in the Room script:

This is from nodes/room.gd

```
var room_type : Types.rooms
var room_position : Vector2i
var sanctuary_side : Types.room_neighbors

func get_neighbor_positions() -> Dictionary:
    return {
        Types.room_neighbors.top: Vector2i(room_position.x, room_
        position.y - 1),
        Types.room_neighbors.right: Vector2i(room_position.x + 1, room_
        position.y),
        Types.room_neighbors.bottom: Vector2i(room_position.x, room_
        position.y + 1),
        Types.room_neighbors.left: Vector2i(room_position.x - 1, room_
        position.y),
    }
```

```
func get_neighbor_position(neighbor : Types.room_neighbors) -> Vector2i:
    return get_neighbor_positions()[neighbor]

func has_neighbor(neighbor : Types.room_neighbors) -> bool:
    var neighbor_position = get_neighbor_position(neighbor)
    return Variables.room_positions_taken.has(neighbor_position)

func get_neighbor(neighbor : Types.room_neighbors) -> GameRoom:
    var neighbor_position = get_neighbor_position(neighbor)

    for next_room in Variables.rooms:
        if next_room.room_position == neighbor_position:
            return next_room

    return null

func free_side() -> int:
    for neighbor in Types.room_neighbors.values():
        if not has_neighbor(neighbor):
            return neighbor
    return -1
```

These are all helpers we can use to work out whether there are rooms or could be rooms around this one. We need this for a couple of reasons:

- When we're generating the grid of rooms and need to figure out the available spots

- When we're showing or hiding arrows and sanctuaries

That first part looks like this:

This is from nodes/globals/generation.gd

```
func make_rooms(parent) -> void:
    # ...snip

    var rooms_left = Constants.number_of_rooms - 1

    Variables.room_positions_available += first_room.get_neighbor_
    positions().values()
    Variables.room_positions_taken.append(first_room.room_position)
    Variables.rooms.append(first_room)
```

```
Variables.room_positions_available.erase(
    Variables.room_positions_available[randi() % Variables.room_
    positions_available.size()]
)
```

We find all the neighbor positions and add them to the list from which we'll generate the next room. Before we do that, we remove one of the potential neighbor positions. We want to have a sanctuary in the first room. This will be on the "free side."

Now, we need to build the rest of the rooms. Each room follows a similar creation process, though they're positioned off-screen.

This is from nodes/globals/generation.gd

```
func make_rooms(parent) -> void:
    # ...snip

    Variables.room_positions_available.erase(
        Variables.room_positions_available[randi() % Variables.room_
        positions_available.size()]
    )

    while rooms_left > 0:
        var next_room_position = Variables.room_positions_available[randi()
        % Variables.room_positions_available.size()]
        Variables.room_positions_available.erase(next_room_position)

        var next_room_type : Types.rooms

        if rooms_left == 1:
            next_room_type = Types.rooms.last
        else:
            next_room_type = Types.rooms.other

        var next_room = Constants.room_scene.instantiate() as GameRoom
        parent.add_child(next_room)
        next_room.room_position = next_room_position
        next_room.room_type = next_room_type
        next_room.position = Vector2(-999, -999)
```

Can you guess why we need to store the available room positions and created rooms? We need these in the Room helper methods, or we could have used local variables. We're also setting the types of most of the rooms to other and the last one to last.

The final bit of code needs to set the sanctuary side of the first and last rooms and fetch any new potential room positions:

This is from nodes/globals/generation.gd

```
func make_rooms(parent) -> void:
        # ...snip
        next_room.position = Vector2(-999, -999)

        if next_room_type == Types.rooms.last:
            var free_side = next_room.free_side()
            next_room.sanctuary_side = free_side

        Variables.room_positions_taken.append(next_room_position)
        Variables.rooms.append(next_room)

        for neighbor_position in next_room.get_neighbor_positions().
        values():
            if not Variables.room_positions_taken.has(neighbor_position)
            and not Variables.room_positions_available.has(neighbor_
            position):
                Variables.room_positions_available.append(neighbor_
                position)

        rooms_left -= 1

    var free_side = first_room.free_side()
    first_room.sanctuary_side = free_side
```

Be sure to check out the sample project code for this full listing, since it's too large for me to include here. We can now remove the instance of Room we manually placed in PlayScreen and call the make_rooms method to dynamically place rooms:

This is from nodes/screens/play_screen.gd

```
extends GameScreen

@onready var _stage := %Stage as Control

func _ready() -> void:
    Generation.make_rooms(_stage)
```

The only way to see this code in action, before the player can walk around in them, is to open the remote debugger. If you run the game and then look above the node tree, you'll see a *Remote* and a *Local* button.

When you're designing, then you should be looking at the *Local* view. If the game is running and you'd like to see the nodes and their values, then you can click *Remote* and inspect things.

Inspecting rooms in the remote view

Hiding Invalid Arrows and Sanctuaries

Before we add player movement, let's clean up the look of the rooms by hiding invalid sanctuaries and arrows. Let's define a new Room method for this:

This is from nodes/room.gd

```
@onready var _sanctuaries := %Sanctuaries as Node2D
@onready var _arrows := %Arrows as Node2D

func hide_invalid_stuff() -> void:
    for node in _sanctuaries.get_children():
        node.visible = false

    for node in _arrows.get_children():
        node.visible = false

    for side in ["top", "right", "bottom", "left"]:
        var name = side.capitalize()

        if has_neighbor(Types.room_neighbors[side]):
            _arrows.get_node(name).visible = true

        if [Types.rooms.first, Types.rooms.last].has(room_type):
            if sanctuary_side == Types.room_neighbors[side]:
                _sanctuaries.get_node(name).visible = true
```

It's interesting that we can use square-bracket syntax on enums, giving us the ability to use a dynamic string. We need to call this method in the generation code:

This is from nodes/globals/generation.gd

```
var free_side = first_room.free_side()
first_room.sanctuary_side = free_side

for room in Variables.rooms:
    room.hide_invalid_stuff()
```

Moving Around in the Rooms

We're going to add click-to-move navigation. This means putting into practice some things we learned in Chapter 8.

Let's create a player character, based on some of what we learned:

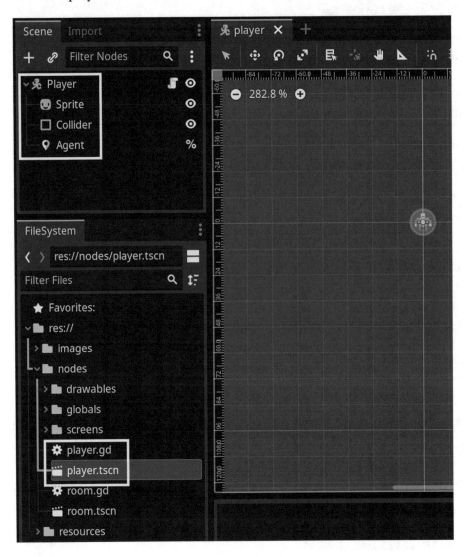

Setting up the player

This Player node consists of the following things:

- It is a CharacterBody2D node.

- It has a Sprite2D node for visuals.

- It has a CollisionShape2D node to work out collisions.

- It has a NavigationAgent2D node to work out pathing.

The code for it differs from the code we wrote previously. We're using the NavigationAgent2D node to calculate a path, and we're using that path in a different way. It still works as expected, but now we have a bit more control over what we do with the path information.

Here's the code in a format that's easier to read:

This is from nodes/player.gd

```
extends CharacterBody2D
class_name GamePlayer

@onready var _agent := %Agent as NavigationAgent2D

var speed := 1000

func _ready() -> void:
    _agent.velocity_computed.connect(
        func(safe_velocity : Vector2) -> void:
            velocity = safe_velocity
            move_and_slide()
    )

    _agent.set_target_location(global_position)

func _unhandled_input(event: InputEvent) -> void:
    if event is InputEventMouseButton:
        if event.is_pressed():
            _agent.set_target_location(event.position)
            _agent.get_next_location()

func _physics_process(delta: float) -> void:
    if not _agent.is_navigation_finished():
```

```
var target := _agent.get_next_location()
velocity = global_position.direction_to(target) * speed
_agent.set_velocity(velocity)
```

Go through each of the scenes and make sure that all the nodes with green icons have their *Mouse Filter* settings to *Ignore*. This is so that the _unhandled_input method is called on the GamePlayer class, without the other controls intercepting it.

Another important thing to note is that we must call the get_next_location method at least once so that the NavigationAgent2D node can determine whether the navigation is finished. We continue to call it inside the _physics_process method so that the path can update if colliders move.

Remember to check the *Avoidance Enabled* check box so that the velocity_ computed signal is emitted.

We also need to change the Room scene so that it has navigation data and injects a player into the first room:

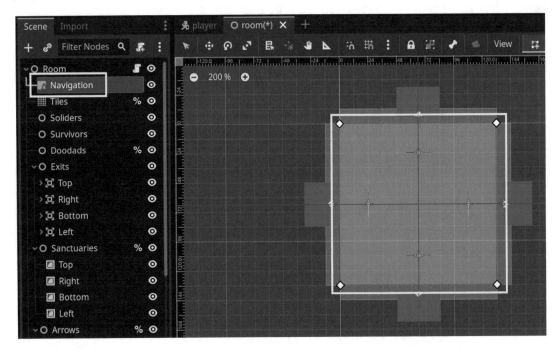

Adding navigation mesh data to Room

This is a NavigationRegion2D node, with a custom rectangle of navigation data drawn into the Room. Chapter 8 explains this in a bit more detail, but the gist is that this area is used to calculate where NavigationAgent2D nodes can navigate.

We can inject the GamePlayer node through the PlayScreen scene:

This is from nodes/screens/play_screen.gd

```
func _ready() -> void:
    Generation.make_rooms(_stage)

    Variables.player = Constants.player_scene.instantiate()
    Variables.rooms[0].add_child(Variables.player)
```

This depends on an exported player_scene reference, so don't forget to also set that up. This code adds it to the first room. The player is also stored in a variable on the Variables global so that we can get it from within the rooms.

Launch the game and click around a bit. You should see the step layer move to your cursor.

Transitioning to Neighboring Rooms

It's time we added the ability to move between rooms. In the beginning of the chapter, we added Area2D nodes that would serve as the doorways between rooms. We're now going to put them to use.

When the player's body collides with the exits, we want to start the transition into another room. The trouble is that they can't just be added to the new room in the same position, or they'll trigger the transition in that room as well.

We need to disable all the colliders so that only one transition happens. Let's add the colliders to groups so that we can disable them without a lot of traversal code:

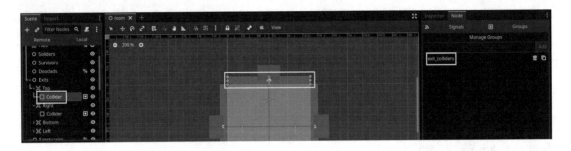

Adding nodes to groups for bulk actions

Next, let's build a function to move the player from their current room to the new room:

This is from nodes/room.gd

```
func add_player(side : Types.room_neighbors) -> void:
    call_deferred("disable_colliders")
    await get_tree().create_timer(0.1).timeout

    var old_room = Variables.player.get_parent()

    if old_room:
        old_room.remove_child(Variables.player)
        old_room.position = Vector2(-999, -999)

    position = Vector2(-66, -66)
    add_child(Variables.player)

    Variables.player.reposition(get_spawn_position(side))

    await get_tree().create_timer(0.1).timeout
    call_deferred("enable_colliders")
func disable_colliders() -> void:
    get_tree().call_group("exit_colliders", "set_disabled", true)

func enable_colliders() -> void:
    get_tree().call_group("exit_colliders", "set_disabled", false)

func _on_top_body_entered(body : PhysicsBody2D) -> void:
    if not body is GamePlayer:
```

```
        return

    var from_side = Types.room_neighbors.top

    if has_neighbor(from_side):
        get_neighbor(from_side).add_player(Types.room_neighbors.bottom)
func _on_right_body_entered(body : PhysicsBody2D) -> void:
    if not body is GamePlayer:
        return

    var from_side = Types.room_neighbors.right

    if has_neighbor(from_side):
        get_neighbor(from_side).add_player(Types.room_neighbors.left)
func _on_bottom_body_entered(body : PhysicsBody2D) -> void:
    if not body is GamePlayer:
        return

    var from_side = Types.room_neighbors.bottom

    if has_neighbor(from_side):
        get_neighbor(from_side).add_player(Types.room_neighbors.top)
func _on_left_body_entered(body : PhysicsBody2D) -> void:
    if not body is GamePlayer:
        return

    var from_side = Types.room_neighbors.left

    if has_neighbor(from_side):
        get_neighbor(from_side).add_player(Types.room_neighbors.right)
```

The purpose of this function is to take the player from the current room they're in to the next room. We can use the `call_group` method to run a method on every node in the `exit_colliders` group. It runs asynchronously, which means we need to wait for a short time for all the colliders to be disabled.

Godot 3 had a `SceneTree.idle_frame` signal, but I cannot find a suitable substitute for it in Godot 4. This code is the simplest way I could come up with to perform the scene transition.

The only downside is that waiting for a timer is generally not considered a good practice because it opens the code up to potential race conditions. I'm not as concerned about this because I know there are at most eight colliders that we need to disable. It's a quick process.

We could reduce the timeout to something far smaller, and this solution would still work.

If the player is already in a room, then we remove them from it and move it off-screen. We follow this up by adding them to the next room and position it in the center of the screen. We need to connect the body_entered signals of each Area2D to the listener methods we've defined here.

We also need to define those reposition and get_spawn_position methods, so let's start with the latter:

This is from nodes/room.gd

```
@onready var _spawns := %Spawns as Node2D

func get_spawn_position(neighbor : Types.room_neighbors) -> Vector2:
    var spawn_name := Types.room_neighbors.keys()[neighbor].capitalize()
    as String
    var spawn_node := _spawns.get_node(spawn_name) as Marker2D

    return spawn_node.position
```

This method is a shortcut for finding the named Spawns → Marker2D node and returning its position. Here's what the reposition method looks like:

This is from nodes/player.gd

```
func reposition(new_position : Vector2) -> void:
    position = new_position
    _agent.set_target_location(global_position)
    _agent.get_next_location()
```

We could expose the _agent variable so that other classes could set these properties manually. But the NavigationAgent2D's target is linked to the GamePlayer's position, so this helper makes sense.

Since we have the add_player method, we can use it when we add the player to the first room:

This is from nodes/screens/play_screen.gd

```
func _ready() -> void:
    Generation.make_rooms(_stage)

    Variables.player = Constants.player_scene.instantiate()
    Variables.rooms[0].add_player(Types.room_neighbors.top)
```

The player will now spawn at the same position as the Top Marker2D node. When they move transition to a room above their current one, they'll be positioned at the Bottom Marker2D node.

Spawning Survivors

A game about rescuing survivors needs survivors to rescue. Let's make a little survivor node and then spawn it into some of the rooms. It's like the player's character:

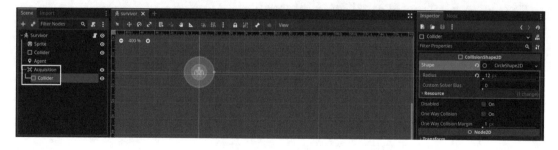

Setting up the Survivor node

We need another Area2D node to act as the acquisition radius. When the player enters this radius, the survivor will attach themselves to the player. They'll continue to follow the player until they reach the sanctuary.

The Room node can be responsible for spawning these survivors. The best place to spawn them would be on top of a grass node, since these should always be navigable. Alternatively, you could create a new pixel color for the spots survivors should spawn.

We can also start the Survivor script off with most of the code in the Player script:

This is from nodes/survivor.gd

```
extends CharacterBody2D
class_name GameSurvivor

@onready var _agent := %Agent as NavigationAgent2D

var speed := 1000

func _ready() -> void:
    _agent.velocity_computed.connect(
        func(safe_velocity : Vector2) -> void:
            velocity = safe_velocity
            move_and_slide()
    )

    _agent.set_target_location(global_position)

func _physics_process(delta: float) -> void:
    if not _agent.is_navigation_finished():
        var target := _agent.get_next_location()
        velocity = global_position.direction_to(target) * speed
        _agent.set_velocity(velocity)

func reposition(new_position : Vector2) -> void:
    position = new_position
    _agent.set_target_location(global_position)
    _agent.get_next_location()
```

To allow the survivors to spawn on grass drawables, we need to make the layout available to other methods:

This is from nodes/room.gd

```
var layout : Array

func _ready() -> void:
    layout = Generation.get_room_layout()

    Generation.add_room_tiles(_tiles, layout)
    Generation.add_room_doodads(_doodads, layout)

    spawn_survivors()
```

The spawn_survivors method we follow this up with needs to randomly select a grass tile for the survivor spawn:

This is from nodes/room.gd

```
@onready var _survivors := %Survivors as Node2D

func spawn_survivors() -> void:
    var used_coordinates : Array[Vector2i] = []

    for i in randi_range(Constants.minimum_survivors_in_room, Constants.
    maximum_survivors_in_room):
        var survivor := Constants.survivor_scene.instantiate() as
        GameSurvivor
        _survivors.add_child(survivor)

        var coordinates = Vector2i(randi() % Constants.layout_width,
        randi() % Constants.layout_width)
        var drawable_type = layout[coordinates.y][coordinates.x]

        while drawable_type != Types.drawables.grass or used_coordinates.
        has(coordinates):
            coordinates = Vector2i(randi() % Constants.layout_width,
            randi() % Constants.layout_width)
            drawable_type = layout[coordinates.y][coordinates.x]

        used_coordinates.push_back(coordinates)

        survivor.reposition(coordinates * Constants.sprite_width)
```

This includes three new constants:

- `Constants.minimum_survivors_in_room`
- `Constants.maximum_survivors_in_room`
- `Constants.survivor_scene`

I'll leave it to you to set these up. After creating the GameSurvivor instance, we keep attempting to select an unoccupied position for them. Once found, we can spawn the survivor.

Rescuing Survivors

The last thing we're going to do together is give the survivors more functionality:

- They should be able to follow the player.
- We should allow them to move between rooms.
- The player should be able to drop them off at the sanctuary.

GameSurvivor already has an acquisition Area2D node, so we can tie into the signal emitted when a body enters it:

This is from nodes/survivor.gd

```
var following : GamePlayer

func _on_acquisition_body_entered(body : Node2D) -> void:
    if body is GamePlayer:
        body.survivors.push_back(self)
        following = body

func _on_follow_timer_timeout() -> void:
    if following:
        _agent.set_target_location(following.global_position)
```

I've attached a signal listener to the Survivor's Acquisition node, in which I check if the body entering is a player. If so, I set the following variable to the player instance.

You'll also notice I created a timer, called FollowTimer. The timeout signal is useful for updating the survivor's NavigationAgent2D target location. The timer is set to *Autostart* and is not set as a *One Shot*. This means it will start automatically and keep timing out.

Don't forget to add a `survivors` array to the player class, where we can store references to survivors following the player.

When we launch the game, we're greeted by an unfortunate side effect of the current `NavigationAgent2D` system. Nested `Area2D` and `CollisionShape2D` nodes will be included in the avoidance detection logic.

This means that we cannot actually get inside the acquisition radius to acquire the survivor.

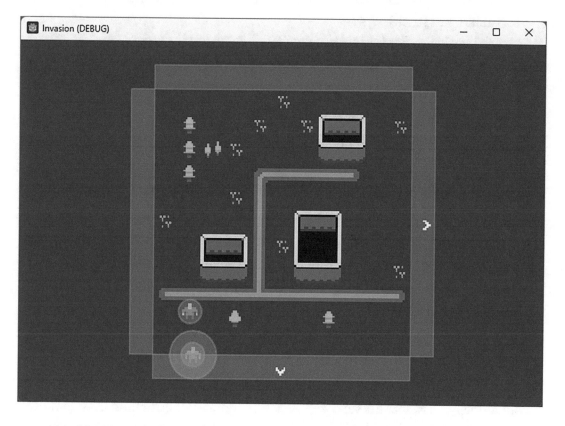

Nested `CollisionShape2D` nodes interfering with collision avoidance

I could have skipped over this part by going straight to the alternative. I chose, instead, to highlight this issue because it's likely to cause you a lot of headaches if you don't know it's there.

One solution to this problem is not to use an Area2D node to detect acquisition. We can use the distance from the player's position to the survivor's position:

This is from nodes/survivor.gd

```
@onready var _follow_timer := %FollowTimer as Timer

var following : GamePlayer

func _on_follow_timer_timeout() -> void:
    if not following and Variables.player.global_position.distance_
    to(global_position) < 50:
        following = Variables.player
        Variables.player.survivors.push_back(self)

    if following:
        _agent.set_target_location(
            following.global_position
        )
```

We can delete the Acquisition Area2D node, since we don't need it anymore.

I also spent some time fiddling with the Survivor → Agent *Path Desired Distance* and *Target Desired Distance*. I arrived at 5 pixels being a good setting for both of these. Since we're not controlling the survivors, it's ok if they aren't as responsible or accurate as the player.

These increased values mean their movement will be smoother and their targeting more forgiving.

Additionally, I saw that the survivors were sometimes hidden behind the doodads. I moved the Doodads node above the Survivors node so that they display above the doodads.

We can make the survivors move to different rooms in the same method we use to allow the player to transition to different rooms:

This is from nodes/room.gd

```
func add_player(side : Types.room_neighbors) -> void:
    call_deferred("disable_colliders")
    await get_tree().create_timer(0.1).timeout

    var old_room = Variables.player.get_parent()

    if old_room:
        old_room.remove_child(Variables.player)
        old_room.position = Vector2(-999, -999)

        for survivor in Variables.player.survivors:
            survivor.get_parent().remove_child(survivor)

    position = Vector2(-66, -66)
    add_child(Variables.player)

    Variables.player.reposition(get_spawn_position(side))

    for survivor in Variables.player.survivors:
        _survivors.add_child(survivor)
        survivor.reposition(Variables.player.global_position)

    await get_tree().create_timer(0.1).timeout
    call_deferred("enable_colliders")
```

We need to remove the survivors from their parent before we can add them to the new room. Remember, they're children of the Survivors node, so we can't remove them from the room. If we added them to a group, then we can use the call_group method instead of needing to find their parents.

Once the player is in the new room, we can add the survivors to the new room. Since we can now take survivors back into our starting room, we can rescue them:

This is from nodes/room.gd

```
func _on_top_body_entered(body : PhysicsBody2D) -> void:
    if not body is GamePlayer:
        return
```

```
    var from_side = Types.room_neighbors.top

    if room_type == Types.rooms.first:
        rescue_survivors(from_side)

    if has_neighbor(from_side):
        get_neighbor(from_side).add_player(Types.room_neighbors.bottom)
func _on_right_body_entered(body : PhysicsBody2D) -> void:
    if not body is GamePlayer:
        return

    var from_side = Types.room_neighbors.right

    if room_type == Types.rooms.first:
        rescue_survivors(from_side)

    if has_neighbor(from_side):
        get_neighbor(from_side).add_player(Types.room_neighbors.left)
func _on_bottom_body_entered(body : PhysicsBody2D) -> void:
    if not body is GamePlayer:
        return

    var from_side = Types.room_neighbors.bottom

    if room_type == Types.rooms.first:
        rescue_survivors(from_side)

    if has_neighbor(from_side):
        get_neighbor(from_side).add_player(Types.room_neighbors.top)
func _on_left_body_entered(body : PhysicsBody2D) -> void:
    if not body is GamePlayer:
        return

    var from_side = Types.room_neighbors.left

    if room_type == Types.rooms.first:
        rescue_survivors(from_side)

    if has_neighbor(from_side):
        get_neighbor(from_side).add_player(Types.room_neighbors.right)
```

```
func rescue_survivors(side : Types.room_neighbors) -> void:
    if side != sanctuary_side:
        return

    for survivor in Variables.player.survivors:
        Variables.player.survivors.erase(survivor)
        survivor.queue_free()
```

This looks like a lot of code, but that's only because there is some repetition for the different Area2D signals. The gist of it is that we have some special functionality if the current room is the first room.

If the player is in the first room and they are on the sanctuary side, then all the survivors following them are rescued.

We could collapse this code even further by using a common signal method, but that's a bit more complicated than I want to make this code.

Taking Things Further

This is where we stop working on this project together, but there's still loads more you can do to it. Here are some features that will bring it closer to my original build of Invasion:

1. Have a visual indicator that appears when you are close to a survivor, for how close you need to be to get them. In my version, I used a yellow circle, so the player can see how close they must get to the survivor.

2. Show how many survivors there are to rescue, somewhere on the screen, and track how many have already been rescued.

3. Spawn soldiers, and have them patrol between random road drawables. They can have a similar indicator for how close you can get to them before they start to chase you.

4. Add a dialog system to display conversations between the player, soldiers, and survivors.

5. Have a hope counter, which continually drains but can be increased when you rescue a survivor.

6. If soldiers catch you while you have no following survivors, decrease the player's hope.

7. If soldiers catch you while you have following survivors, make them detain the survivors. You can decide what the hope penalty is for these, so it might be more favorable to be caught alone or with company.

8. Add an exit transition, and populate the summary screen with data about the current state of hope.

9. Add a game-over transition for when hope has completely run out.

Summary

This has been an ambitious chapter, wherein we built the majority of the functionality for Invasion. It's not exactly what I released, but it includes everything fundamental. It gives you a good jumping-off point for customization and novel mechanics of your own.

I am so proud of what we've covered in this chapter and the book as a whole. This is our third game, and it showcases the majority of what I'd consider practical procedural content generation. I encourage you to take your time with this chapter and project. If you feel like there are topics that you don't have a handle on, spend some time going over the code and researching specifics in the Godot community.

If you can produce a game like Invasion, you're ready to use these skills in your own games.

In the following chapter, we're going to look at generating and adhering to stricter paths of movement. This will be useful for games where you want richer NPC movement or less free player movement.

CHAPTER 11

Paths and Path Followers

We've discussed moving the player with keyboard and mouse input. Depending on the game, these might allow for too much freedom. What if we want to make experiences that are more "on rails"?

In this chapter, we're going to explore the ins and outs of path-based movement. We'll create a basic path follower, followed by more complex chain pathing.

Defining Paths

Let's create a new experiment, called `PathsExperiment`, and set it as the experiment that loads on `PlayScreen`. We'll populate it with a `Path2D` node, a `PathFollow2D` node, and a `ColorRect` node for visibility:

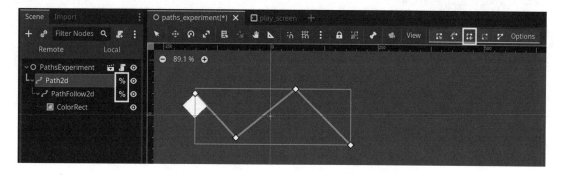

Setting up to follow paths

You can draw the path in the same way that you'd draw a collision polygon. Select the `Path2D` node and click the *Add Point* button to start drawing path points.

If you were to create a `PathFollow2D` node, not as a child of a `Path2D` node, you'd see an error. This is because `PathFollow2D` nodes only work as children of a `Path2D` node.

© Christopher Pitt 2023
C. Pitt, *Procedural Generation in Godot*, https://doi.org/10.1007/978-1-4842-8795-8_11

PathFollow2D nodes have a *Progress* property, which represents the distance along the path that the follower has moved. It starts at zero, but as you increase that value, you'll see the follower move along the path.

They also have a *Progress Ratio* property that represents the distance along the path they have travelled, but as a value between 0 and 1. As you change one of these sliders, the the other will change to match.

As you can imagine, it's possible to tween the progress values.

Moving Along the Path

Imagine we want to allow the player to click somewhere near the path and have the player character move to the nearest point along the path.

To do this, we'd need to first work out what the nearest point is. We'd need to be able to tell whether it was "forward" or "backward" path movement. Then, we could animate the movement until the player character was around the path point.

Let's figure out the first bit:

This is from experiments/paths_experiment.gd

```
extends GameExperiment

@onready var _path := %Path2d as Path2D

var debug_points := []

func _unhandled_input(event: InputEvent) -> void:
    if event is InputEventMouseButton:
        if event.is_pressed():
            var nearest_point = get_nearest_point(event.position)

            debug_points.append(nearest_point)

            await get_tree().create_timer(5.0).timeout
            debug_points.erase(nearest_point)

func _process(delta: float) -> void:
    queue_redraw()

func get_nearest_point(target : Vector2) -> Vector2:
    return _path.curve.get_closest_point(target)
```

```
func _draw() -> void:
    for point in debug_points:
        draw_circle(point - global_position, 10, Color.BLACK)
```

I've chosen to draw little black dots at the nearest point along the path. When the player clicks on the game screen, we loop through the points of the path. These are not the ones that we used to draw the path, but rather the calculated points in between.

Notice we're using **scene unique names** for the Path2D and PathFolow2D nodes.

We add these to an array, and after a five-second delay, we remove them again. Adding _process and _draw methods allows us to draw the dots. The drawing canvas is cleared every frame, so we don't need to do that ourselves. Queue_redraw is a built-in function that forces Godot to call _draw so that our dots show up.

The results are quite pleasing:

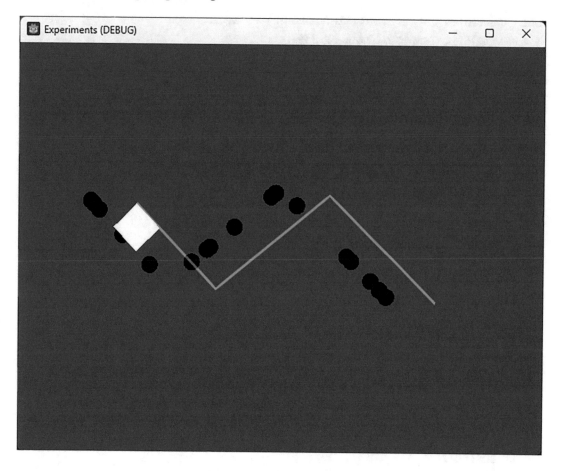

Drawing dots at the closest points to our clicks

The dots are offset a bit, but that's to do with transformations, and it's not a huge deal. Now that we can get the nearest point and actually see it, we can move toward it. Let's define a speed variable and put the movement code in the _process method:

This is from experiments/paths_experiment.gd

```
extends GameExperiment

@onready var _path := %Path2d as Path2D
@onready var _path_follow := %PathFollow2d as PathFollow2D

var debug_points := []
var nearest_point : Vector2
var speed := 200

func _unhandled_input(event: InputEvent) -> void:
    if event is InputEventMouseButton:
        if event.is_pressed():
            var point = get_nearest_point(event.position)

            nearest_point = point
            debug_points.append(point)

            await get_tree().create_timer(5.0).timeout
            debug_points.erase(point)
func move_to_point(target : Vector2, delta : float) -> void:
    var points := _path.curve.get_baked_points()

    var target_i : int
    var current_i : int

    for i in range(points.size()):
        if points[i].distance_to(target) < 5:
            target_i = i

        if points[i].distance_to(_path_follow.position) < 5:
            current_i = i

    if abs(current_i - target_i) > 5:
        if target_i < current_i:
```

```
        _path_follow.progress -= delta * speed
    else:
        _path_follow.progress += delta * speed
func get_nearest_point(target : Vector2) -> Vector2:
    return _path.curve.get_closest_point(target)

func _process(delta: float) -> void:
    queue_redraw()
    move_to_point(nearest_point, delta)

func _draw() -> void:
    for point in debug_points:
        draw_circle(point - global_position, 10, Color.BLACK)
```

The main change is the addition of the move_to_point method, which uses the latest nearest_position as a target to move toward. We loop through the path's points until we find

1. The current follower's point index

2. The target point's index

Knowing these, we can tell if the follower needs to move forward or backward. We can then increase or decrease the follower's offset with delta and speed.

Launch the game and click around. It's wonderful to see the follower try to get as close to your click as possible while sticking to the path.

Moving Between Paths

Following a single path is already cool, but I want to take things a step further. Imagine we want to build maps out of many different paths. In order for a follower to move throughout the whole level, we'd need to allow them to switch between different paths.

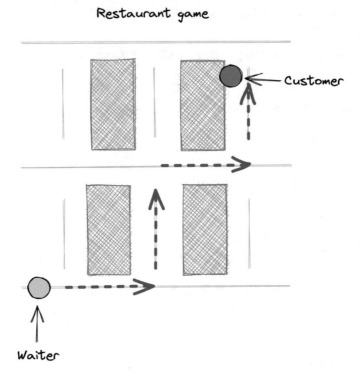

Moving along multiple paths

In this situation, we'd need to be able to link paths together and decide when we want to switch to a new path. The simplest way to link them together would be to create a Path2D subclass that has a property for "connected paths":

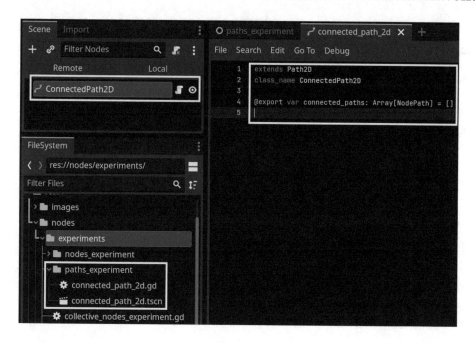

Path2D subclass

We can replace our existing Path2D node with one of these and add a couple more. They have a new *Connected Paths* property that we can use to create the associations between them. If you have trouble drawing separate paths for each ConnectedPath2D node, remove all the points and make the *Curve* properties unique to each ConnectedPath2D.

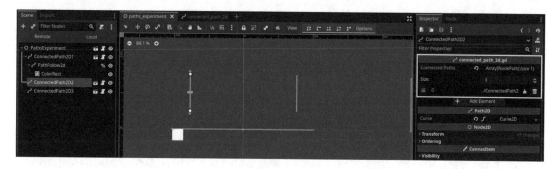

Connecting paths together

Now, our code needs to change. It's going to be simpler to delete all the code in experiments/paths_experiment.gd and start over.

1. Instead of finding the closest point on a single known path, we need to look for the closest point on the closest path.

2. We can calculate which paths to take and how long to travel along them to get to that point.

Let's add a method to address the first task:

This is from experiments/paths_experiment.gd

```
extends GameExperiment

func get_nearest_path(target : Vector2) -> ConnectedPath2D:
    var nearest : ConnectedPath2D
    var distance : float

    for node in get_children():
        if not node is ConnectedPath2D:
            continue

        var point = node.curve.get_closest_point(target)
        var point_distance = point.distance_to(target)

        if not distance or point_distance < distance:
            nearest = node
            distance = point_distance

    return nearest
```

This new method looks through all the ConnectedPath2D nodes in the scene and finds the one with a point that is closest to the click. This gives us the target path we want to travel to, so we need to work out a way to get onto that path.

Next, we need to find a list of points that will take the PathFollow2D node from the path it is on to the path closest to the click target.

This happens in a few steps:

1. We look through each of the connected_paths set for the starting path.

2. If one of them is the end (we're right next to the path we want to be on), then we get the coordinates between start and end.

3. If not, we add start and end nodes to the sequence array so that they are part of the journey the PathFollow2D node will take.

4. For each of the sequences (there can already be multiple if the starting path was connected to multiple other paths), we get the last element and loop through its connected paths.

5. If we get a connection that is already part of the sequence we're inspecting, we ignore it. This is to prevent us from going backward.

6. We carry on with this process until we find the path closest to our target.

This is from experiments/paths_experiment.gd

```
func get_waypoints(start : ConnectedPath2D, end : ConnectedPath2D)
-> Array:
    var sequences := []

    for connected in start.connected_paths.map(func(p): return start.get_
    node(p)):
        var pair = [
            start,
            connected,
        ]

        if connected == end:
            return add_coordinates_to_waypoints(pair)

        sequences.push_back(pair)

    while sequences.size() > 0:
        var sequence = sequences.pop_front()

        var last = sequence[sequence.size() - 1]
```

```
        for connected in last.connected_paths.map(func(p): return last.
    get_node(p)):
            if sequence.has(connected):
                continue

        var appended = sequence + [connected]

        if connected == end:
            return add_coordinates_to_waypoints(appended)

        sequences.push_back(appended)

    return []
```

add_coordinates_to_waypoints adds metadata to each waypoint, or step in the journey:

This is from experiments/paths_experiment.gd

```
func add_coordinates_to_waypoints(route: Array) -> Array:
    var entries := {}

    for path in get_children().filter(func(node): return node is
    ConnectedPath2D):
        for connected in path.connected_paths.map(func(connected): return
        path.get_node(connected)):
            var nearest_path_point : Vector2
            var nearest_connected_point : Vector2
            var nearest_distance : float

            for path_point in path.curve.get_baked_points():
                for connected_point in connected.curve.get_baked_points():
                    var distance = path_point.distance_to(connected_point)

                    if not nearest_distance or distance < nearest_distance:
                        nearest_path_point = path_point
                        nearest_connected_point = connected_point
                        nearest_distance = distance

            entries[str(path.get_instance_id()) + "-" + str(connected.get_
            instance_id())] = {
```

```
                "leave": nearest_path_point,
                "enter": nearest_connected_point,
            }

    var new_waypoints := []

    for i in route.size():
        var current = route[i]

        var waypoint = {
            "node": current,
        }

        if i > 0:
            var previous = route[i - 1]
            var key = str(previous.get_instance_id()) + "-" + str(current.
            get_instance_id())

            new_waypoints[i - 1].leave = entries[key].leave
            waypoint.enter = entries[key].enter

        new_waypoints.push_back(waypoint)

    return new_waypoints
```

This code creates four loops to generate a lookup table of all the closest join points for each direction. entries will contain data resembling

- "path1-path2": { enter: Vector2(1, 1), leave : Vector2(1, 2) }

- "path1-path3": { enter: Vector2(3, 1), leave : Vector2(3, 2) }

- "path2-path1": { enter: Vector2(1, 2), leave : Vector2(1, 1) }

- "path3-path1": { enter: Vector2(3, 2), leave : Vector2(3, 1) }

leave is the position at which the follower leaves the path that it is on, and enter is the position at which it enters the new path. We can use this to plot the course from where the follower is to where it needs to be, via jumps between paths.

This transforms a simple array of steps into an array of instructions:

1. From the current path 1

2. Go to position x on path 1

3. Join onto path 2

4. Go to position y on path 2

5. Join onto path 3

6. And so on

All that's left to do is create a new `move_to_point` method so that it moves to the point nearest that last click (if we're on the right path) or moves to the exit and exits the current path:

This is from experiments/paths_experiment.gd

```
@onready var _path_follow := %PathFollow2d as PathFollow2D

var nearest_path: ConnectedPath2D
var nearest_point: Vector2
var waypoints: Array
var speed := 200

func _unhandled_input(event: InputEvent) -> void:
    if event is InputEventMouseButton:
        if event.is_pressed():
            nearest_path = get_nearest_path(get_local_mouse_position())
            nearest_point = get_nearest_point(nearest_path, get_local_
            mouse_position())
            waypoints = get_waypoints(_path_follow.get_parent(),
            nearest_path)

func get_nearest_point(nearest_path: ConnectedPath2D, target : Vector2) ->
Vector2:
    return nearest_path.curve.get_closest_point(target)

func _process(delta: float) -> void:
    move_to_point(delta)
```

```
func move_to_point(delta : float) -> void:
    var current_path = _path_follow.get_parent()

    var target_i : int
    var current_i : int

    var points = current_path.curve.get_baked_points()
    var target : Vector2

    if waypoints.size() < 1 or current_path == waypoints.back().node:
        target = nearest_point
    else:
        target = waypoints.filter(func(w): return w.node == current_path).
        front().leave

    for i in range(points.size()):
        if points[i].distance_to(target) < 5:
            target_i = i

        if points[i].distance_to(_path_follow.position) < 5:
            current_i = i

    if abs(target_i - current_i) > 3:
        if target_i < current_i:
            _path_follow.progress -= delta * speed
        else:
            _path_follow.progress += delta * speed

    elif waypoints.size() > 0 and current_path != waypoints.back().node:
        for i in waypoints.size():
            if waypoints[i].node == current_path:
                var next_path = waypoints[i + 1].node

                current_path.remove_child(_path_follow)
                next_path.add_child(_path_follow)

                move_to_offset_position(waypoints[i + 1].enter)
func move_to_offset_position(target : Vector2) -> void:
    while target.distance_to(_path_follow.position) > 5:
        _path_follow.progress -= 1
```

As mentioned, if we're on the right path, then the target position is the curve point nearest the click. If not, we actually want to move toward where we exit the current path and enter the next path.

When the follower is near enough to exit the current path, we switch the follower over to the new path and change its progress until it is close to where it can to enter the new path.

Summary

In this chapter, we took a deep dive into how to set up `Path2D` nodes and their companion `PathFollow2D` nodes. We explored how to animate the movement of a follower on a single path and between paths.

This might seem like a lot of work for little benefit, but it's a useful trick for the kind of game we're going to finish this book building. More on that later.

CHAPTER 12

Interaction Systems

Before we wrap up our journey together, I'd like to spend a bit of time talking about how we enable interactions between players and the world.

In this chapter, we're going to look at how to handle proximity-based interactions and how to display interactions when they happen.

It's a little difficult to show these concepts without the context of a game, because they are so dependent on the specifics of the game; but we'll try anyway.

I'll talk through different code approaches, but I don't expect you to create a dedicated experiment for the concepts in this chapter. The approach you take will definitely depend on the game you're building.

Managing Interactions

Think back to when we made our own version of Invasion. The player can move through the map, encountering survivors.

© Christopher Pitt 2023
C. Pitt, *Procedural Generation in Godot*, https://doi.org/10.1007/978-1-4842-8795-8_12

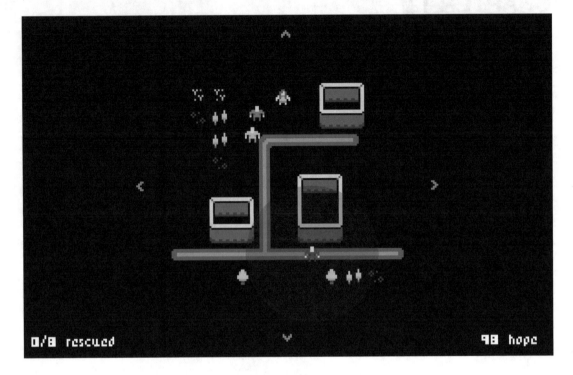

Interacting with survivors

The way we coded it was that the survivors would immediately start to follow the player when they were close enough to each other. We could make the game a lot deeper by giving the player a choice to rescue or abandon the survivor.

One practical way to do this would be to use Area2D nodes to detect the approach of the player. If the player is in range of something that can be interacted with, we can present them with a prompt to let them know that interaction options are available. Many games do this, including one of my favorites:

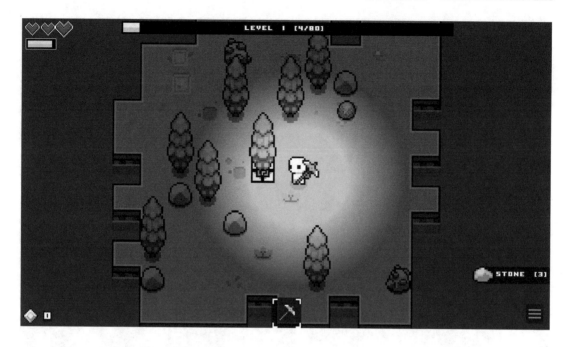

Interacting with things in Forager

In Forager, when you are close enough to interact with something, it gets this square indicator. Sometimes, you'll need to press a specific button to begin the interaction. Other times you'll be able to whack at the tree or stone with the tool you're holding.

The way I usually code this sort of thing is to have a dedicated node, called Interactable:

Making a reusable interaction manager

These Area2D-based nodes should have their collision layers and masks set to a layer dedicated to this purpose.

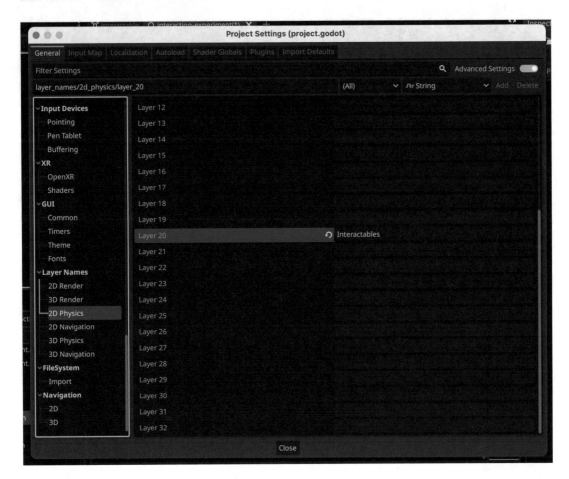

Setting an unused layer for interactables

The base Interactable node doesn't have a collision shape or collision polygon defined, because this should be set as it is added to another node.

Keeping it simple, we can use a `CollisionShape2D`:

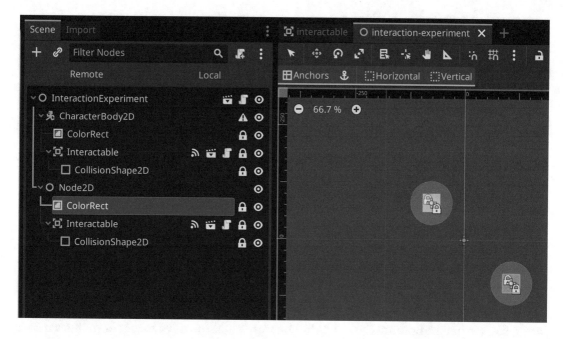

Creating an example to assess functionality

If we were to switch to remote view while running code like this, we'd see the *Other Interactable* variable is null:

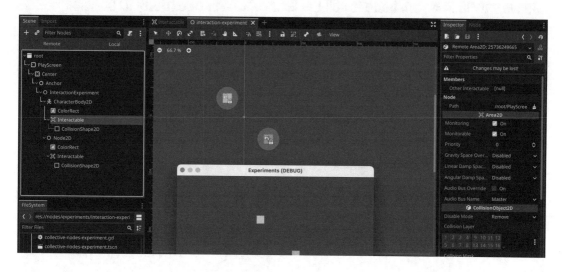

Not collisions...

If we then moved the player so that it collided with the NPC, we'd see the link created:

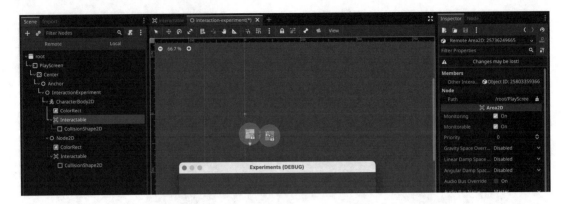

...Until we move the player closer

At this point, we could show that interactions are possible. If the player pressed the appropriate key, we could even cause the interaction to begin.

The way the player moves closer depends on the game. It could be via keyboard input, like we had in Bouncy Cars. It could be from click-to-move navigation, like we had in Invasion. The point is that the collision detection and behavior are no longer in the players' scripts, but rather in a dedicated node.

As we saw in Invasion, there is still the issue of `CharacterBody2D` collision shape avoidance preventing us from using arbitrary `Area2D` nodes in this way. We'd need to change the survivors to not be `CharacterBody2D` nodes if we wanted to retrofit this interaction model on to Invasion.

Since we're using signals, we can attach listeners to run code when the signals are emitted. A signal for receiving the interaction (from Player → NPC) could show a new conversation or start some NPC code:

Handling initiated interactions

If we wanted to show that interaction was possible, even before the player presses a key to start the interaction, we could add more signals to Interactable:

```
extends Area2D
class_name Interactable

signal interactable_entered(other)
signal interactable_exited(other)
signal receive_interaction(me)

var other_interactable : Area2D = null

func initate_interaction() -> void:
    if other_interactable != null:
        other_interactable.receive_interaction.emit(self)

func _on_interactable_area_entered(interactable : Area2D) -> void:
    other_interactable = interactable
    interactable_entered.emit(interactable)

func _on_interactable_area_exited(interactable : Area2D) -> void:
    interactable_exited.emit(interactable)
    other_interactable = null
```

How This Could Apply to Invasion

Let's think about how this approach might work if we added it to Invasion. The screenshot I showed earlier was from my first build of the game and is a bit more feature-rich than the version we built together.

If it already includes soldiers and when you get close enough to them, they chase you down. You can escape them by moving to another screen. If they catch you and you have a survivor already following you, then the survivor freezes in place and you can no longer rescue them.

I didn't have an interaction system in the original version of Invasion, but if I had to add one, I might try the following:

- Allowing the player to decide whether they rescue survivors they encounter. Perhaps some survivors will slow the player down or cost the player something to rescue. Allowing the player to make the decision to rescue would be more interesting than the survivor immediately following the player.

- Allowing the player to decide what to do when a soldier catches up to the player. Could you choose what happens to the survivor? Could you keep the survivor by giving the solider something else? What if a currency spawned inside the map and you could trade it for safe passage?

Having Conversations

A common way for interactions to happen in games is for the main characters to have conversations. This could be a detective asking questions during an investigation, or a boss monologging before their untimely demise.

The original version of Invasion included dialog between the player, survivors, and soldiers:

Conversations with survivors

On spawning, I assigned each soldier and survivor with a portrait. When the player walked in range of a survivor, I'd select and play a random survivor line. When a soldier caught up to the player, I'd play a random soldier line.

I handled all the dialog with a third-party add-on, called Dialogic. You can find the add-on and installation instructions over at GitHub. There's also a companion website, with links to documentation:

Dialogic website

Dialogic has a custom editor, which allows you to preconfigure different conversations. The interface changes from time to time, but it should resemble this layout:

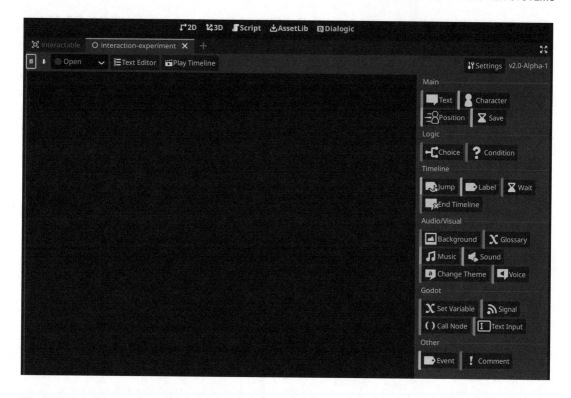

The Dialogic interface

This is where you can create new conversations, with custom portraits, sound, and decision trees. There's a lot of depth to this add-on, but I want to focus on the simplest of setups.

There are some steps to showing dialog:

- You need to create a few characters.

- You need to set up timelines.

- You can start a timeline with the `Dialogic.start_timeline` method.

I thought it might be useful to show you what I did for the first version of Invasion, so you have a sense of what's possible.

Dialog in Invasion

I followed the first two steps in that list so that I had a full set of characters and some example timelines for my game:

Setting up characters and timelines

It's worth noting that this screenshot is from Godot 3.x and Dialogic 1.x. The interface and methods with which we start timelines will be different to Godot 4.x and Dialogic 2.x.

As you can see, there are a ton of soldier profile pictures, around 30 in total. I created the soldier profile pictures with a red hue and then re-colored them to yellow for the survivor profile pictures.

The example timelines were a sequence of events and text that model the typical dialog structures I wanted for Invasion:

Creating example timelines

Dialogic has methods we can use to play these timelines. Playing a pre-created timeline is ok, but I wanted to achieve something a bit more dynamic. Fortunately, these timelines are saved in text files, and inspecting them allowed me to set up dynamic conversations:

```
68 ⌄ func show_acquired_dialog(survivor_character : Dictionary) -> void:
69  ⟩    randomize()
70
71  ⟩    show()
72
73  ⟩    current_dialog = Dialogic.start("")
74  ⟩    current_dialog.connect("dialogic_signal", self, "on_dialogic_signal")
75
76 ⌄ ⟩  current_dialog.dialog_node.dialog_script = {
77 ⌄ ⟩ ⟩    "events":[
78 ⌄ ⟩ ⟩ ⟩    {
79  ⟩ ⟩ ⟩ ⟩        "action": "join",
80  ⟩ ⟩ ⟩ ⟩        "character": survivor_character.file,
81  ⟩ ⟩ ⟩ ⟩        "event_id": "dialogic_002",
82  ⟩ ⟩ ⟩ ⟩        "mirror": false,
83  ⟩ ⟩ ⟩ ⟩        "portrait": "",
84 ⟩⟩ ⟩ ⟩ ⟩        "position": { ▱
90  ⟩ ⟩ ⟩ ⟩        }
91  ⟩ ⟩ ⟩    },
92 ⌄ ⟩ ⟩ ⟩    {
93  ⟩ ⟩ ⟩ ⟩        "character": survivor_character.file,
94  ⟩ ⟩ ⟩ ⟩        "event_id": "dialogic_001",
95  ⟩ ⟩ ⟩ ⟩        "portrait": "",
96  ⟩ ⟩ ⟩ ⟩        "text": acquire_survivor_lines[randi() % acquire_survivor_lines.size()],
97  ⟩ ⟩ ⟩    },
98 ⌄ ⟩ ⟩ ⟩    {
99  ⟩ ⟩ ⟩ ⟩        "action": "leaveall",
100 ⟩ ⟩ ⟩ ⟩        "character": "[All]",
101 ⟩ ⟩ ⟩ ⟩        "event_id": "dialogic_003",
102 ⟩ ⟩ ⟩    },
103 ⌄ ⟩ ⟩ ⟩    {
104 ⟩ ⟩ ⟩ ⟩        "emit_signal": "hide",
105 ⟩ ⟩ ⟩ ⟩        "event_id": "dialogic_040",
106 ⟩ ⟩ ⟩    },
107 ⟩ ⟩    ],
108 ⟩  }
109
110 ⟩    _background.add_child(current_dialog)
```

Dynamic conversations

A lot of this data is what I call "magic variables," inasmuch as they're static internal values that Dialogic understands. The interesting thing is that creating these timelines dynamically means we can substitute the characters and lines at runtime.

In this version of Invasion, I randomly selected the soldier and survivor profiles when the soldiers and survivors were added to each room. Remembering what each survivor looks like means we can show the same profile pictures for them over the course of a level.

Summary

I hope you have a better sense of some of the things you can add to your games, which will help them feel more immersive and interactive. I'm sure they will be useful in the final game we're going to make.

CHAPTER 13

Recreating This War of Mine

We've come a long way, and it has all led to this final project. It's time to challenge yourself by building a game on your own. It's a game you're capable of building if you've been following along.

In this chapter, I'm going to explain how I would recreate another popular game. You're free to follow my guidance, or to deviate if you can think of a better approach or mechanic for your version.

This War of Mine

This War of Mine is a game in which you are again trying to survive in a besieged city. That's where the similarity with Invasion ends. It's a beautiful 2D simulation strategy game, in which you try to feed and comfort the people under your roof.

© Christopher Pitt 2023
C. Pitt, *Procedural Generation in Godot*, https://doi.org/10.1007/978-1-4842-8795-8_13

Surviving in a broken house

It's a somber and often hopeless setting and a punishing game. You spend much of the game making the best out of bad situations. Despite the setting, This War of Mine is a masterpiece of game design and implementation.

The primary resources are food, medical supplies, defensive equipment, and building materials. The player plays by selecting a character and moving them somewhere to perform an action.

- Characters can only interact with something when they get close enough to it.

- Characters can navigate to it by walking along floors and up stairs or ladders.

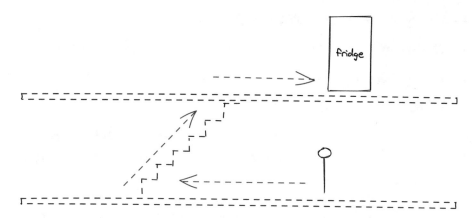

Navigating the house

There are other types of levels, but I want to focus on this main one because it's where you spend most of your time. Each new game begins with a randomly generated house and a selection of survivors.

The survivors you begin with determine the difficulty you will have. Some survivors have illnesses or dependencies on rare resources. There are also modes where you get a random selection of survivors.

Let's focus on these mechanics for our version:

- Random starting survivors

- Random house generation

- Movement through the house

- Interaction with house repairs, eating food, resting, looting

- Hunger and hope meters for each survivor

You can, of course, choose to implement more or fewer of these. I'll suggest how I would do it, but the actual implementation is up to you.

Getting Set Up

I'd begin by creating the base Screen scene and inheriting from it for the following screens:

- Main menu screen

- Settings screen

- New game screen (save slot management)

- Play screen

- End-of-day summary screen

- End-of-game summary screen

This kind of game doesn't need a win condition. "Survive for the longest time" is enough of a goal. If you want to limit that at a certain number of days, then you'd also need a winning summary screen.

You're already familiar with how to set the UI elements up for this screen. Start with the usual `MarginContainer`, `CenterContainer`, `VBoxContainer`, and various other controls. Then, check out themes for your UI elements.

Custom themes are inherited, so you can save the theme as a resource and link it to every parent control node. The child control nodes will have the theme automatically applied:

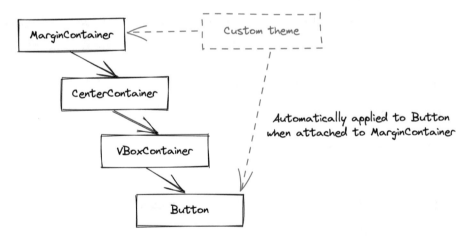

Nested controls inherit themes

I'd use the `Screens` global, along with screen transitions, as we did when recreating Invasion. I might also tinker with a different shader effect. I'm no expert, but there are plenty of shaders to be found on the Godot Shaders website.

We haven't spent any time talking about how to generate sounds, because it's not been the focus of this book. That doesn't mean sounds are unimportant. At this point, I'd make some menu music or look for some menu music and sounds to play when the player clicks on a menu button.

If you're looking to use someone else's sounds, I recommend checking out these places:

- `https://opengameart.org/content/library-of-game-sounds`

- `https://itch.io/game-assets`

You can find a wide selection of free game assets to use on these websites. If you'd prefer to make your own, then I can recommend

- `https://sfxr.me`

- `https://sfbgames.itch.io/chiptone`

- `https://famistudio.org`

- `www.audacityteam.org`

If you're looking for advanced tools, search for "Digital Audio Workbench." They are usually quite pricey, though.

You can buy music and sound effects from many websites if you don't want to make it. I tend to get my premium artwork, music, and sound effects from Envato's sites:

- `https://audiojungle.net`

- `https://graphicriver.net`

While we're on the subject, these are tools you can use for making graphics for your games:

- `www.piskelapp.com`

- `www.aseprite.org` (not free, but recommended)

If you're looking for more free game assets, don't forget about Kenney's website.

Generating Levels

When generating levels, I'd stick to the approach we've been using. You can create pixel art layouts for each different room and render them as tiles or nodes. We don't need to plan out the whole level – only uniformly sized rooms that we can randomly place in room slots.

It might be a bit more tricky if you want to misalign the rooms on each floor. In that case, the layout image should contain options for whole floors.

There's still plenty you can do to randomize the layout inside each floor. You can use the collective nodes we learned about while making Invasion. You can even mirror the floors or rooms.

Into those floor layouts, I'd dedicate a special pixel color for points on a path so that we can map the walkable area. When drawing the floors or rooms, we could create a Path2D or a NavigationRegion2D for the characters to move along.

If you are sticking to path-based navigation, this is how that could work:

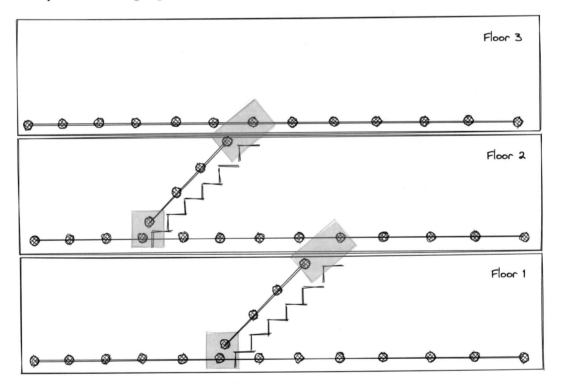

Navigating along Path2D nodes

We learned about paths in Chapter 11, so refer to that for a refresher. We don't actually need to create the links between the Path2D nodes, either. The approach we learned about finds the closest points between two paths and travels through them.

Some levels in This War of Mine feature rooms that are closed off until a character clears a path or picks a lock. We can achieve this by creating separate paths blocked by nearby doors:

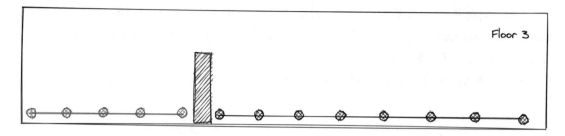

Conditionally available paths

We can define a "door" pixel and a different "path" pixel that creates a path automatically disabled until an adjacent door is cleared.

While disabled, the path shouldn't be navigable. I expect you'll have to bring it into or out of certain groups and filter on those groups when you're looking for available paths to traverse.

More advanced stuff, to be sure.

Selecting Starting Characters

A big part of what makes This War of Mine replayable is the variety of characters you can start with and gain.

You could spend a lot of time building this part of the game:

- You can add hope, hunger, and health to each character, but...

- Some characters can have lower or higher starting values for these.

- Feeding certain foods or performing certain activities can increase or decrease these values.

- Feeding certain addictive resources can cause addiction (like coffee, cigarettes, etc.).

- Keeping characters with addictions "topped up" can give them more hope or less hunger than usual.

- Failing to provide these resources to characters can cause their hope or health to drain faster.

There's no limit on what you can add to these systems; and managing them is a major focus of This War of Mine. I'd suggest you decide the features you want to add up front and stick to implementing those.

Scope creep can kill your project at this point.

Interacting with Objects in the World

As we learned in Chapter 12, we can achieve interaction using Area2D nodes near to each other. This could be an interactable node attached to the fridge or a door or a bed. If the characters can move within the range of the object, then they might be able to interact with it.

This War of Mine sometimes requires characters to "open" containers before being able to loot them using tools and time.

You might want to think about the conditions in which characters may interact with things:

- A bed needs to be vacant for a character to sleep.

- A cupboard needs to be openable before a character can loot it.

- You need enough food to be able to cook.

- You need the correct building materials to be able to repair a broken wall.

All these interactions can contribute to the general well-being of each character:

- Characters that sleep can heal and regain some hope or lose some tiredness.

- Characters that eat can lose hunger.

- All characters living in the house can gain some hope when one of them repairs part of the house.

This War of Mine also has randomized events that happen overnight, such as break-ins and attacks. The more you repair the house, the less frequent or severe they tend to be. That's an interesting mechanic!

Ending the Day

After a set amount of time, the day should end. This is a good time to remind the player how they are doing and to start random events or allow characters to leave the house.

We should show an end-of-day screen. This can display days survived, remaining food, and a general summary of the health and hope of the current characters.

You can decide whether to deduct a fixed amount of hunger at this point, or do so during the day. The length of the day is also something you get to decide, since it won't match the passage of time in the real world.

Deciding When to End the Game

There are many ways you could decide the player has won or lost the game. I'd go with the following set of criteria:

- When a character's hope gets to zero → they leave in the night.
- When a character's health gets to zero → they die.
- When there are no more characters in the house → the game is over.

We can determine the final score based on how long the characters have survived for and how many good things they did while in the house. When characters interact with each other in a positive way, or do things to enrich the lives of other characters, we can count this as a good thing.

This "good things" system might be overkill. I'm throwing ideas out there for you to think about.

All that is to say, the game must end. When it does, you can show the game-over summary screen.

Unlocking New Levels and Characters

You can encourage players to replay your game by allowing them to unlock new levels and characters after having played a certain way or for a certain amount of time.

The point isn't to force them to grind. It should be a nice reward for immersing them in a dystopia; and it will allow them to try new styles of play.

You can make the unlocked levels larger or longer or with more random events. You can even represent these new levels on an interactive map:

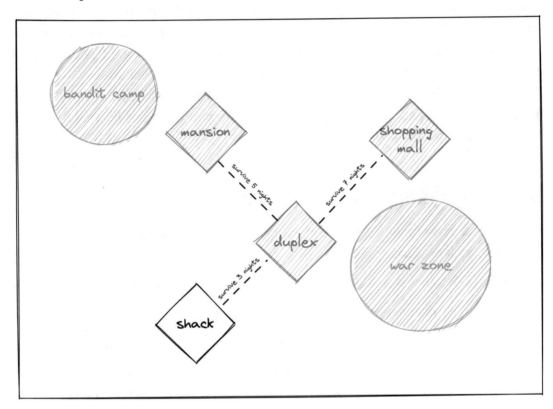

Select where you want to live

Allowing the player to choose the challenge

A Note About Mobile Game Development

It's no accident that the games we have built could mostly work on a touch screen. I am a fan of building games that can work well on a touch screen because those are the kinds of games I like to make for my kids.

You can build this game without ever needing the player to type something, or otherwise press a button on a keyboard. If you manage to keep this approach, you'll also be able to publish your game to Android and Apple tablets and phones.

I have published many games to these platforms, and it's a wonderful feeling being able to play a game you've made on a mobile device you own.

It's also why I have used `MarginContainer` as the main node for my screen scenes. You can adjust the margins of `MarginContainer` to account for phone buttons, notification areas, and notches.

It's a bit more work to support different screen sizes, but it's worth it for the joy players will get from being able to play your games on the devices they have on hand.

Taking It One Step at a Time

It's easy for me to sit here and tell you how I would build this game, when you are the one who has to build it. Indie game development can sometimes feel like you're wearing all the hats and nobody is helping.

Take things one step at a time.

Start with a small scope, create a task list, give yourself a deadline. Then, begin the process of cutting scope or deprioritizing non-essential features so that you can launch on time.

For every game I've published, five more concepts have died. I'm talking as much to myself as I am to you. Keep at it and you can realize your dreams of making games you and your friends and family can enjoy.

Thank You for Reading This Far

It's time I got going. I want to thank you for reading through this book. I hope it's been as much fun for you to follow along as it was for me to write. This was my first book as an indie game developer, so I'm sure there is room for improvement.

I want to echo what I said before. If you have questions, or things aren't working, then please reach out to me and ask questions. I love talking about this stuff, and it's the least I can do to point you in the right direction.

Twitter: assertchris

Email: cgpitt@gmail.com

Index

A

AtlasTexture, 65

B

Bouncy Cars, 169, 176, 182, 228
  bit masks, 115
  configuration, 100
  constants code, 98
  coop racing game, 95
  draw_map() function, 114
  map drawing, 112–116
  map generation
    cell types/pixel colors, 105, 106
    clockwise/anticlockwise
      direction, 107, 108
    corner layout, 105
    get_map method, 109–112
    multidimensional
      array, 106, 110
    source code, 108
  menu nodes, 99
  player movement, 125–128
  player nodes, 96, 97
  players drawing, 116–121
  road tiles, 115
  rotate_players method, 119
  screen node, 96–98
  seed-based generation
    extension filter, 104
    game screen, 102

NewGame screen, 105
phrase node, 105
text file, 103
stretch settings, 102
vertical alignment, 99
warning message, 129–131
waypoints calculation
  firing bullets, 123
  map information, 122
  source code, 123–125
  waypoint arrow, 129
window size, 101

C, D, E, F

Collective nodes
  approaches, 151
  appropriate node, 154, 155
  memory refreshing, 151–153
  Node2D code, 154
  OptionButton nodes, 152
  tile map variations, 154

G

Godot 4 project, 11
  blank project creation, 11, 12
  configuration, 17
  GameScreen class, 14, 15
  loading experiment project
    @export/@onready variables, 20
    GameExperiment class, 18

C. Pitt, *Procedural Generation in Godot*, https://doi.org/10.1007/978-1-4842-8795-8

L, M

N, O

Printed in the United States
by Baker & Taylor Publisher Services